Our Charleston

Lowcountry Photos, People and Places

Volume II

Published by

The Post and Courier

A Division of The Evening Post Publishing Company
Larry Tarleton, Publisher

ISBN 978-0-615-25271-1

Printed by
Inland Graphics
U.S.A.

Family Outing, 1912

Eight family members are set to take the Franklin out for a drive in 1912. The family lived at 34 Smith St., a home Julius H. Jahnz purchased in 1902 for $10,000.

Continued on page 38.

Submitted by Mary Lou Coombs

Paving SC 61, 1930s

Edward E. Anderson, wearing overalls, a necktie and hat, was working for the county as chief mechanic in the mid-1930s when he prepared the roadbed for paving Highway 61.

Continued on page 55.

Submitted by Raymond Anderson

The Wave, 1935

Sarah King (left) and her friend, Mary Collette, nicknamed "Ting," lived on Yonges Island but often enjoyed socializing at Folly Beach. The girls attended St. Paul's High School and were about 17 years old at the time of this photo, in 1935.

Submitted by Nancy Smoak Peeples

On the Cover

FOREWORD

Lowcountry residents love to talk about the past. We'll strike up a conversation with total strangers and tell them about our great-grandmother's recipe for she-crab soup, or how our uncle, three generations back, fought in the recent unpleasantness. Charlestonians will speak with reverence about the Holy City and its churches, some of the first in the nation, or with a wink in their eye when they share tales of the more raucous days of this seaport community.

We like to celebrate and we don't need much cause to do so. Beyond weddings, births and holidays, we find immense joy in family outings. Give us a clear day, some sweet tea and a place to gather and we'll share memories, retell stories and remember those people who paved the way to our unique lifestyle.

We are strong in our faith, diverse in our character and resolute in our pride. Undeniably, we like to share, and that's what "*Our* Charleston, Lowcountry Photos, People and Places" (Volume II) is all about.

The following pages contain hundreds of photographs contributed by readers of The Post and Courier. They were collected from family albums and Bibles, hope chests and places of prominence in Charleston homes, so that we may share with you our remembrances of Lowcountry life from the 1800s through 1960.

Robie Scott, *Editor*
"*Our* Charleston, Lowcountry Photos, People and Places" (Volume II)

Special effort was made to ensure accuracy of information accompanying these photographs.
However, information written on the backs of photographs and dates recalled by contributors may
not have been exact. For historical accuracy, we welcome corrected/additional information.
It will be forwarded to the appropriate archives, museums and editors. Additionally, if you have
Lowcountry photos you would like to contribute for upcoming volumes, please write to:

Our Charleston
Robie Scott
134 Columbus St.
Charleston, S.C. 29403-4800

Notes from Volume I:
Page 27 – Photo titled "Grandmother's Pride and Joy," was taken in 1908 as noted by Franz D. Cone.
Page 101 – Photo titled "Birthday Party on The Beach," Betty Craig (Rivers) Lewine's name was listed incorrectly as noted by Elizabeth Rivers Lewine.
Page 101 - "Birthday Party on The Beach" the names Derrill Maybank (now Mrs. Ben Hagood) and Anne Ford Melton were listed incorrectly as noted by Anne Ford Melton.
Page 126 – Photo titled "Let's Play Ball," Hamlin Farms was incorrectly listed as Hamlin Plantation as noted by Elizabeth Hamlin McConnell.

ACKNOWLEDGMENTS

Our Charleston, Lowcountry Photos, People and Places, Volume II

The Project Staff

Robie Scott, *Editor*

Jamie Drolet, *Retail Advertising Manager*

Krena Lanham, *Sr. Graphic Designer*

Lisa Foster, *Writer*

Jason Clark, *Classified Advertising Art Director*

Tamara Murray Wright, *Retail Advertising Art Director*

Libby Wallace, *Data Desk Editor*

Lathornia Perry, *Librarian*

Pam Liles, *Librarian*

Shannon McCarty, *Advertising Graphic Designer*

Danny Enfinger, David Fields Sr., Dan Riddle, Jerry Lee Thomas Jr., Jason Baxley,
Frankie Lee, Jason Price, Sherry Delany, Dennis Anderson, *Imaging/Scanning*

Special Thanks

Barbara Williams

Christine Randall

Elizabeth Flynt

Zach Norris

Early Charleston Dairy

John and Lena Mindermann had 45 cows at their dairy and residence on Cannon Street. Raw, unpasteurized milk was produced and delivered by the people with pushcarts, shown in the photo. When an ordinance was passed making it illegal to keep cows in the city, the dairy moved across the Ashley River and later ceased operations.

Submitted by George B. Alexander

1800s – 1900s

Christmas Portrait ▲

The holidays were an occasion for family gatherings, to share food, fellowship and presents. Family and friends celebrated at Theodore Melchers' home, 105 Drake St., in 1897. Theodore is in the back holding a baby. Theodore's son, William, is in front of the Christmas tree with his wife, the former Lily Caroline Welling, to his left. Theodore's father-in-law, the Rev. Ludwig ("Louis") Mueller, pastor of St. Matthew's Lutheran Church, is to the right of the tree with the mutton chop whiskers.

Submitted by Franz D. Cone

The Mindermanns ▼

John Mindermann and his wife, Lena (Sturcken) Mindermann, pictured below, owned a dairy at 61 Cannon St. in the late 1800s. Their daughter Gertrude married Burton Augustus Alexander from Summerville and the couple had 13 children.

Submitted by George B. Alexander

American Ingenuity Success Story ▼

In the late 1800s Walter Moore began a business in the back yard of 8 George St. that became known as Moore Drums. Over the years he and his brother reconditioned wooden drums and barrels, crates, boxes, bags, croaker sacks and feed bags which were then sold as shipping containers. Rice was a huge export at that time; even the rice hulls were retained to use as packing material around china being shipped in Moore's barrels to England. In the late 1920s steel drums entered the market.

Submitted by Jack Moore

Cotton Farmer ▲

Glenn William Reeves was a farmer of "King Cotton" and a substantial landowner in the Givhans-Edisto River area at the turn of the century. He was born in 1812 and died just 10 days before his 84th birthday. He was about 78 years old in this photo, taken in 1890.

Submitted by Ruth Clark

Proud German Heritage ◄

Brothers Franz Hermann, Theodore Anton Wilhelm and Alexander Josephus Melchers (left to right) arrived in Charleston in 1848; their sisters Maria Anna ("Jenny") and Agnes Bertha Melchers (left to right) arrived two years later. All three brothers were Confederate captains. After the war, Franz returned to his earlier occupation as the editor of the *Deutsche Zeitung*, Charleston's German newspaper. Alexander opened a bakery on King Street, and Theodore had a wholesale grocery store on the corner of Queen and East Bay streets. Jenny married Henry Bischoff and Agnes married Richard Issertel.

Submitted by Franz D. Cone

The Ghostly Griffin Place, Jedburg ▶

According to the current owner, there is a rumor that Mr. Griffin's ghost rambles around the 150- to 200-year-old house. Before carpeting the hall, the tapping sound of his cane could be heard. The sound always stopped at the foot of the stairs. On many occasions the family has heard a ticking clock in the wall of the den and bedroom, and the living room chandelier swings back and forth at times when there is no air movement. It sways for several minutes before stopping on its own.

Submitted by Ruby Browning

Wando Summer Home ▲

This residence, built in the 1800s, was W.C. Tharin's summer home. In those days people owned plantations in Mount Pleasant and kept a summerhouse right on the river. Wando was a small village at that time, comprised of just a few families. A sand road led up to the house where family gathered for Sunday picnics and the children went crabbing and shrimping.

Submitted by Elizabeth Huguley

Citadel Square Baptist Choir ▲

J. H. Linsebrink was a paid tenor in the Citadel Square Baptist Church choir around 1859. He is pictured on the back row, third from the left. In addition to being an accomplished singer, he also was a cabinet maker.

Submitted by Lisa L. Longshore

Pastor's Wife ◄

Caroline Laurent Mueller was married to the Rev. Ludwig (Louis) Mueller, pastor of St. Matthew's German Evangelical Lutheran Church. The church, located at 405 King St., was organized in 1840 to serve members of the German-speaking Charleston community. Mrs. Mueller was born in Zweilbrucken, The Palatinate, in what is now Germany.

Submitted by Franz D. Cone

The Johnson Family ◄

Sarah A. (Wienges) Johnson, pictured in the center, recorded family details in a Bible that was given to her Jan. 1, 1861. In the late 1890s the family Bible was more than a sacred document; it was an historical account. According to her Bible, Sarah was born on June 8, 1842. She died at 1:35 p.m., Saturday, June 25, 1910 at 14 John St. Their children were Precious (seated on the left), Capers (standing behind her), Eva (seated on the right) and Louisa (standing).

Submitted by Precious Gregory

Wedding Photo, 1900 ◄

Viola G. A. Fuseler married John F. E. Meyer, Sr. on Wednesday evening, Dec. 12, 1900. The ceremony took place at 87 Church St., the home of the bride's parents, Henry W. and Mina Wolfe Fuseler. The residence was acquired by The Charleston Museum when Henry W. Fuseler died in 1929. Known as the Heyward-Washington House, it was opened the following year as Charleston's first historic house museum, according to the museum website.

Submitted by Kimberly Meyer Lewis

Pompion Hill Chapel ▲

Eugene Noble Simons worshipped at his ancestors' church and took this photo of the parishioners April 30, 1922. Services are still held twice a year at Pompion Hill Chapel on the east branch of the Cooper River. The original wooden church, built in 1703, was the first Anglican church outside of Charleston. That structure was replaced by the current one-story Georgian brick church in 1763, which was built on the same site. It remains much as it was when the building was completed in 1765: no electricity, with a pulpit of red cedar.

Submitted by Carlton Simons

Music Instructor

Professor Fritz Daurer and his wife are pictured in this studio photograph around the 1870s. Professor Daurer was from Germany and taught music to South Carolina Governor Manning's children.

Submitted by Lisa L. Longshore

The Manito

The Manito was built in 1892 for Edward Alexander Simons. She is flying the Carolina Yacht Club flag and won several competitions under those colors in the late 1890s. She is pictured here in the Charleston harbor with a three-masted sailing ship in the background.

Submitted by Carlton Simons

Puckhaber Brothers Band △

In the late 1880s the Puckhaber family belonged to the German Artillery, a militia organization similar to the Washington Light Infantry. The German Artillery Hall was located on Wentworth Street between King and Meeting streets but all that remains today is the iron rail fence around the Gibbes Museum of Art on Meeting Street. It was the German Artillery that fired the salute when President Teddy Roosevelt visited Charleston for the South Carolina West Indian Exposition in 1901. The Puckhabers seated (left to right): George L., John F. and Herman F. Puckhaber. The Puckhabers standing (left to right): John H., Henry H. and William H. Puckhaber.

Submitted by George Puckhaber

The Simons Children

Sara (Simons) Hastie, born Nov. 1, 1892, and her brother Edward A. Simons, Jr., frame the face of their mother, Sarah (Simonds) Simons, in 1894. Sarah lost her son to dysentery in 1895; she died two years later aboard the SS St. Louise between New York and Southhampton, England. Mrs. Simons was traveling to Germany for health reasons.

Submitted by Carlton Simons

Formal Affair ◀

Margaret Francis Maguire, age 11, was probably dressed for her confirmation day in 1897. Maggie's father, M.E. Maguire, was an engineer on a ferryboat that ran between Charleston and Mount Pleasant. The Maguires lived in a row house at the north end of Wentworth Street; the houses are still in existence.

Submitted by Tom McLaughlin

Four Mile House ▼

Named because it was four miles from the courthouse downtown, the Four Mile House on Meeting Street was the last roadside inn in lower South Carolina. Dating back to 1786, the old house was demolished in 1969 despite Preservation Society efforts to save it. Attempts were made to move the house to another location; those attempts failed due to overhead power line obstruction.

Submitted by Charles Christopher Brandt

The Witt Family

Meta Mohring Witt, pictured here with her children around 1893, had lost her husband Louis Witt some five years earlier. Mrs. Witt bought 504 Meeting St. in 1906 and she and her son Fred (second from left) ran a grocery there. Her daughters Lena (left) and Mamie Anna helped out as well. On the back of this photo, taken at Clarke's Photo Studio at 265 King St., the photographer offers to enlarge the photo to any size and finish in crayon if desired.

Submitted by Carl Sohl

Horres Daughters ▲

May Frances (left), Alice Estelle and Lillian Horres were the daughters of John Jacob and Alice Estelle (Turner) Horres. The family lived on Hanover Street. Mr. Horres operated a wood yard in 1893, when this photo was taken.

Submitted by Carl Sohl

19th Century Merchant Marine ▲

Leon Joseph Oliver immigrated from the northern coast of Spain and took up residence in Charleston as a merchant marine in the late 1800s. It was a difficult way to earn a living, with no laws in place to protect crewmen from abuse by officers, and no legislation regulating safety, pay or quality of food. Seamen were required to have no real qualifications; they didn't even have to speak the same language. According to legislation passed in 1915, the Seamen's Act mandated at least 75 percent of the ship's crew must be able to understand the language spoken by its officers.

Submitted by Donna Thomas

Claussen's Bakery Founder ▲

Johann Christian Heinrich Claussen and his wife are pictured on their golden wedding anniversary in 1897. Claussen, a German immigrant, established Claussen's steam bakery in Charleston.

Submitted by Lisa L. Longshore

The "Golden Glow" ▲

The cottage, built by Stephen Thomas in the 1800s, was used as a summer retreat from Charleston heat. The Thomas family, like many others, took the ferry to Mount Pleasant and caught the trolley from there to Sullivan's Island, stopping at Station 23. Original glass, china doorknobs and footed tubs survived everything except Hurricane Hugo in 1989, when the storm twisted the home on its foundation.

Submitted by Claudia FitzGerald

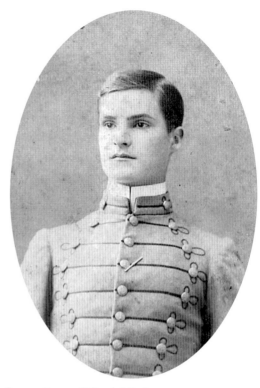

Generations of Citadel Cadets ▲

The de Saussure men have attended The Citadel since 1842, skipping only one generation. Dr. Henry W. de Saussure was a knob in 1890; after graduation he attended the Medical College of South Carolina and did post-graduate work in Boston and Atlanta. His career led him into the field of obstetrics and gynecology but he was also a surgeon and the city physician.

Submitted by Mary McQueen

German Schüetzenfest ▲

The Charleston Rifle Club held a shooting contest every year at Ashley Park. The "Schuetzenfest," which is German for "Marksmen Festival," allowed men only to participate in marksmanship, but there was plenty to keep the whole family entertained, including colorful floats and a chance to dress up. Pictured here around 1903 are Daisy Owens Fischer and William Daniel Fischer with their children William, Daisy and Elma. Mr. Fischer is wearing his marksmanship medals.

Submitted by Margaret Wilkes

Sires Residence ▲

The property associated with the home at 328 East Bay St. encompassed a city block, running all the way to the Cooper River. Owners Oscar D. and Blanche Alexander Sires lived there with their five children. Sires, a merchant during the 1900s, partnered with Clarence W. Westendorff to deliver kerosene and artesian water in containers to subscribers, before SCE&G and Charleston Water Works were established. This historic Charleston home is commonly known as Moffett House.

Submitted by LeRoy Sires

Out With the Old, In With the New ◀

John J. Murray was Station Manager for the railroad when this photo was taken, probably at Bennett Yard on the way to North Charleston. Atlantic Coast Line had changed its name to Seaboard Coast Line; both names are represented on the rail cars pictured.

Submitted by Mary Lou Coombs

Old Charleston Home ◄

The Julius H. Jahnz family purchased 34 Smith St. from the Ingrahams in 1902. Originally it was built for George Robertson, a wealthy merchant, in the 1850s. It had a striking view of the Ashley River across Colonial Lake. Jahnz was a co-partner in a hardware distributorship that grew into one of the largest wholesale hardware suppliers in the nation. He also served on the Board of Aldermen. The home is still in existence on the corner of Smith and Beaufain streets.

Submitted by John Coombs

The Welling Family ►

The extended Welling family photo, taken in the summer of 1908, shows the side yard of the address that later became 668 East Bay St. Back row (left to right): William T. Melchers, Eugene Welling, William Ellerbe, Welling Gayer, Herbert Welling, Dorothy Melchers, Evelyn Welling Gayer, Arthur Gayer, Maurice Tiller. Middle row: Frances Welling Ellerbe, holding William Ellerbe, Jr., Lily Caroline Welling Melchers, holding Virginia Dare Melchers, William Russell Welling, Dora Frances Collins Welling, holding Genevieve Tiller, Eloise Doar Welling, holding Marie Welling, Genevieve Welling Tiller. Front row: Emma Welling, Ida Welling, Edwin Welling, Marion Gayer, Eugene Welling, Jr., Margerite Welling.

Submitted by Franz D. Cone

Rosebrock Grocery ◄

Herman Rosebrock, the tall man pictured on the sidewalk, ran a grocery store in the early 1900s on the corner of Logan and Magazine streets. His family joined him out front for the photograph, and also on the porch above, where the Rosebrock residence was located. Although the business sold primarily groceries, the lamps in the window attest to various and sundry consumer goods also offered for sale.

Submitted by Mildred Wieters

The Vennings ▷

In the early 1900s Laura Augusta Edmonston Venning (left) was in mourning for the loss of a daughter. A woman would have worn black for varying periods of time following a death in the family, depending on her relationship to the deceased. Pictured with Mrs. Venning are daughters Mazie (center) and Ella Venning (right).

Submitted by Elizabeth Rivers

West Indian Exposition ▲

This photo, taken sometime between the Dec. 1, 1901 opening of the South Carolina Inter-State and West Indian Exposition in Charleston and its conclusion in 1902, shows some of the magnificent structures and landscaping provided for exhibitors and visitors. The site is now Hampton Park. Mr. and Mrs. Charles T. Tamsberg, Sr. are pictured at the Exposition.

Submitted by Barbara Tamsberg

St. Mary's Girls' School Graduate ◄

Mattie Murphy would have been about 16 at the turn of the century when she graduated from the school run by the Sisters of Charity of Our Lady of Mercy. The school was located in the Nathaniel Russell House and was run by "our" nuns, the nomenclature given to the local girls who devoted their lives to this convent. Mattie is wearing medals for writing and literature. She later married Joe Duane.

Submitted by Mary Coy

74 Spring St. ▲

This charming Victorian home, along with a chest of silver, was presented to Charles and Eloise Welling upon their marriage. The couple lived there until the family of six children, all of whom were born in the house, outgrew those accommodations and moved to King Street. Eloise Doar Welling is holding baby Edwin on the porch; Ida is sitting on the railing with her sister Emma beside her. Eugene is standing by the post and Marguerite is sitting at the top of the stairs.

Submitted by Betty McMichael

714 King St. ▲

When Charles Eugene and Eloise (Doar) Welling needed a larger home, they moved to 714 King St. This residence was built in the early 1900s, probably with the help of Charles' father, William Russell Welling. The area was nothing but a field at that time, and the location was convenient to the family lumber mill. The boy on the fence is Eugene Welling. His mother lived in the house until her death in 1966.

Submitted by Betty McMichael

No Less Bumpy By Bicycle

The wood plank roadway probably would have been no smoother a mode of travel than taking the "bicycle path," or dirt sidewalk, in the early 1900s. William Theodore Melchers is pictured in front of the carriage gate of father-in-law William Russell Welling's home at 86 Bay St. Melchers rented the home in the background, 84 Bay St., from Welling.

Submitted by Franz D. Cone

If You Don't Like the Weather… ▲

It's an old saying: "If you don't like the weather in Charleston, just wait a minute." Magdalene Droze was prepared for a sudden shower in this Clarke's Studio photograph taken around the turn of the century.

Submitted by Peggy Droze

Platform Diving, Circa 1900s ▲

"High diving," as it was called in 1904 when a combination of springboard and platform diving made its debut at the Olympic games in St. Louis, may have been the inspiration behind this diving platform built at Sullivan's Island. Pictured in their wool bathing suits around 1914 those who could be identified are (top left to right): Robert Anderson, Willy Pregnall, Olie Pregnall. Bottom (left to right): Johnnie Weeks, Sallie Anderson, Mr. Aimar and Barnie Baker.

Submitted by Mary Baker Pringle

Charleston Ladies ▲

Sara Glover Wilkinson Waring Simmons, on the right, stands next to Marie Picault Aimar at 139 Ashley Ave. Mrs. Simmons was married to William Clifford Simmons; Mrs. Aimar was the wife of Dr. Charles Pons Aimar, Sr.

Submitted by Mary Tutterow

Woman Entrepreneur

Meta Mohring Witt (center) owned the property at 504 Meeting St. where she ran a grocery business on the street level and lived with her children Fred Henry, Mamie Anna and Lena Margaret on the second floor. Mrs. Witt would have been about 51 years old at the time of this photo. She is pictured in the back yard of her home and business with two unidentified friends.

Submitted by Carl Sohl

Arthur Middleton at the Beach ▼

Three-year-old Arthur appears to be holding the rod of a crabbing net and standing in a bed of seaweed. The family owned a home on Sullivan's Island at Station 11 in 1900.

Submitted by Annely Klingensmith

Showy Chapeaux ◄

"I never did wear fancy hats," Wilhelmina (Patjens) Tiencken used to say. Which begs the question, "What would be considered fancy?" She is pictured here, on the left, with her sister-in-law, Charlotte ("Lottie") (Baum) Patjens, in 1902. The women lived within a stone's throw of each other in Mount Pleasant.

Submitted by Elise Talbert

Moore Drum Beginnings ◄

Walter Allan Moore would have been about 32 years old the year he wed Abbie Lofton. He bought 8 George St. as their family home and established a business of reconditioning wooden drums: rinsing them out and making them water-tight. He sold these barrels to individuals and commercial enterprises as shipping containers. Moore Drum is still in operation on Industrial Avenue.

Submitted by Jack Moore

Ice Is A Hot Seller

The Consumers Ice Company, located on Woolfe Street, ran a pretty good business at the turn of the 20th century under the managerial direction of August W. Wieters. Blocks of ice were delivered by horse-drawn carriage to homes and businesses in downtown Charleston. Consumers was sold to Southern Ice Company in 1924.

Submitted by Mildred Wieters

Buell and Roberts Dry Goods Store ◀

This group of employees from Buell and Roberts, furniture and dry goods dealers, posed for a picture in front of the store about 1898. The store headquartered at 573 and 575 King St. at the corner of Cannon Street.

Front row (left to right): E.D. Andrews, manager of the dry goods department, D.L. Roberts, a member of the firm, Henry Kratzer. Back row (left to right): W.T. Barwich, James P. Brui, Miss Elvina Senicke, Miss Ida Andrews (Mrs. Carl Willard), Miss Jessie Murray (Mrs. James P. Bruce), Miss Lilly Barton (Mrs. Luke Gardner), Miss Carrie Bahr (Mrs. Herbert Boland), Miss Annie White (Mrs. Merino), F. Werner Kracke, Miss Lizzie Coble, Miss Grace Fash (Mrs. Young), William Tylee. The boy could not be identified.

Submitted by Mrs. Cecilia West

Roper Hospital

Bon Secours St. Francis Hospital

A History of Caring

For over 150 years people of the Lowcountry have trusted the name Roper St. Francis Healthcare. You can too.

ROPER HOSPITAL

Recognized for its technology and best practices, Roper Hospital was founded as the first community hospital in the Carolinas. In 1829, Colonel Thomas Roper left $30,000 to the doctors of the Medical Society of South Carolina to treat the sick without regard to complexion, religion or nation. With this gift, the Medical Society established Roper Hospital.

BON SECOURS ST. FRANCIS HOSPITAL

Known for its quality and compassionate care, Bon Secours St. Francis Hospital traces its mission back to Paris and the Sisters of Bon Secours who treated the poor in their homes, going door to door. In 1882, the St. Francis Xavier Infirmary opened as the first Catholic Hospital in South Carolina.

Today more people in Charleston choose Roper St. Francis for healthcare than anywhere else.
Our health system is the area's most comprehensive with two hospitals, four 24-hour ERs and several diagnostic centers.

ROPER
ST. FRANCIS
HEALTHCARE

1910s

Sunday Afternoon Outing

The Bresnihan and Thompson families took the ferryboat over to Sullivan's Island one Sunday afternoon in 1915. Those who could be identified include: (bottom row, far right) William Bresnihan and Rosalee Brandt; (second row, far left) C. Gilmore Thompson and Rena Bresnihan. Nellie Watson is pictured near the top, to the right of the crane and Margaret Speissegger is on the extreme right of the photo.

Submitted by Peggy Droze

Buying Poultry "On Foot" ◄

In the early 1900s the tradition was to never buy a "dead" animal; customers wanted to buy it "on foot," before they took it home to eat. The live turkeys in front of the W.E. Smith Grocery attest to their freshness. William Edward Smith owned the grocery on the corner of King and Shepherd streets; he is pictured in the doorway, wearing a suit. Others pictured in the photo were store helpers. The horse and cart was used to make deliveries to area homes. Mr. Smith died at the age of 44, leaving his wife Bertha with 10 children. She lost the store during the Depression when customers could not pay her the money they owed.

Submitted by Greta Waters

Picnic at Magnolia ▶

Magnolia Cemetery was a favorite "haunt" for picnics in 1918. Every Sunday Ida Welling (left) and Emma Tharin and their families went to the beautiful and peaceful grounds for lunch. The girls were about 13 years old at the time of the photo; they attended Memminger Normal School.

Submitted by Ruth Tharin Smith

World War I Marine Engineers ◄

The proud members of No. 10, most of whom are wearing ribbons and holding flags, were responsible for running "the ships that carry our boys over there" in 1918. Pictured in Marion Square on the first row, fifth from the left, is Thomas Joseph Nolen, Sr., who served aboard a lighthouse tender.

Submitted by Martha Attisano

Ashley Hall Plantation ►

Julius H. Jahnz owned Ashley Hall Plantation in the early 1900s. The property offered plenty of entertainment for Jahnz's eight children (seven girls and one boy), including boating on the Ashley River. Jahnz sold the property to William C. Kennerty several years later. The 1,000-acre plantation dates back to the early 1670s when the land was granted to English settler Stephen Bull.

Submitted by Mary Lou Coombs

New Charleston Mills ◄

Julius Weil, Sr. stands in the doorway of his business at 28 Anson St. around 1915. Weil moved to Charleston in 1913 and shortly thereafter he established New Charleston Mills, a business that made cotton batting. Years later the business changed to making mattresses and was re-named Weil's Mattress Company. The business was at 28 Anson St. for 60 years.

Submitted by Alice Weil

Haute Couture ▶

Catherine (Rena) Bresnihan likely sewed the garment with white fur trim and accompanying hat and muff she is wearing in this photo taken around 1916. She and her mother were accomplished seamstresses and sewed for income as well. Rena was in her mid-twenties at the time and lived on Broad Street.

Submitted by Peggy Droze

Vacation Destination ◄

Marie Saulsbery's family rented a house at Folly Beach for a week every year, back when Folly houses were big, old and $50 a week. Most had at least four bedrooms and a sleeping porch to accommodate several families vacationing together. Marie lived with her grandfather and worked his cotton fields in Givhans until she was 18—old enough to move off the farm and get a job in town at Condon's.

Submitted by Ruth Clark

Charleston Museum Post Card ▲

When Lee Martin, Sr. returned to the states from France in 1919 he sent a note to his sweetheart, Jessie Judy, to let her know he had arrived safely. Martin served in World War I; the couple married about a month later. Charleston Museum took over the Thomson Auditorium at Cannon Park in 1907 and remained there until it burned in October 1981.

Submitted by Merrile M. Kinard

A Handsome Couple ◄

Prior to the marriage of Margaret and Henry Condon, the couple spent a memorable afternoon at Sullivan's Island in 1918. The two are dressed to impress: Margaret in her dapper sailor dress with scalloped hemline and straw hat, and Henry in coat and tie. Henry owned Condon's Baking Company with his brothers at 215-219 St. Philip St.

Submitted by Anne Kingsley

Witt-Gercken Nuptials ▲

Lena M. Witt and E. Henry Gercken were married in 1915 at Lena's mother's home, 504 Meeting St. The family had been members of St. Johannes Lutheran Church on Hasell Street all their lives; Pastor H.J. Black officiated the ceremony. The rug in the background was usually inside the home; it was taken outside when it needed to be cleaned or when it was needed as a photo backdrop. Lena and Henry lived at 504 Meeting St. after the wedding and helped Lena's mother, Meta Mohring Witt, run the grocery store below.

Submitted by Carl Sohl

Happy Couple ◄

Catherine Aloysius Bresnihan was united in marriage with Clarence Gilmore Thompson Wednesday afternoon, April 22, 1914 at the Cathedral of St. John the Baptist.

Submitted by Peggy Droze

High School Football ▽

Porter Military Academy had one of the first high school football teams in Charleston. In 1915 the school was located at the old Federal Arsenal building on Ashley Avenue. Pictured in the first row, second from the left, is Thomas Ritchie Simmons.

Submitted by Mary Tutterow

Harbor Pilot Captain Frank Myatt, Sr. ▲

At the turn of the century a harbor pilot's responsibilities included waiting just beyond the outer jetties and boarding ships sailing into the Charleston harbor, directing the crew through the shipping channels. An outgoing vessel was also extended the same service. But Frank Myatt (left) had duties that went beyond his vocation; he and his wife Lou Teresa Murphy are pictured in 1913 with five of their 18 children. Groceries were purchased by the case. When the family ate meals, Frank ate with the boys in one room and Lou with the girls in another. Pictured on her father's knee is Marguerite, with Genivieve and Leslie standing next to her. Standing on the second row, are Gertrude and Frank, Jr.

Submitted by Bernie Oliver

1917 Kerrison's Window Display ▲

In 1917 Kerrison's sold piece goods and "findings," accouterments such as buttons and ribbons. The window display showed examples of clothing that could be made from these materials. These items would then be fashioned into women's clothing by private seamstresses or Kerrison's employees. The entrance to Kerrison's was on Hasell Street, not on King Street as in later years, because some women patrons refused to be seen shopping. They pulled up in buggies and automobiles while men employed by Kerrison's brought material out to them.

Submitted by Edwin Poulnot III

50-Year Employee ◄

Edwin Huger Poulnot, owner and president of Kerrison's, presented Johnny Bishop (left) with a token of his esteem in honor of 50 years of service with the department store. Bishop was also presented with a crate of chickens in honor of the side business he ran from Kerrison's for many years. Every morning Bishop took orders from store workers for fruits, vegetables and meats; he then went to the city market to make the purchases, and would return and sell the groceries. Bishop worked another 10 years with Kerrison's. The first-floor manager J.C. Lindsey is pictured on the right.

Submitted by Edwin Poulnot III

Cadet Parade Ground or Child Playground? ◄

In 1917 The Citadel was just across the street from Gerald McMahon's home on King Street. He and his friend Benny Berendt always played at Marion Square, and they usually played "soldier." Often Gerald would beg a cap off a cadet and call his "troops" to fall in. Benny responded accordingly. McMahon grew up to coach football and basketball at Bishop England High School.

Submitted by Jerry McMahon

Wadmalaw Islanders ▼

The Townsend family grew up on Wadmalaw Island. Leslie (Townsend) Jervey is pictured here in 1916 with her brothers Thomas, Harry, Charles and Billy.

Submitted by Leslie D. (Sister) Rutledge

Same Wedding Gown, 50 Years Later ▲

When Richard Septimus Venning and Laura Augusta Edmondston Venning married in 1861, just as the Civil War broke out, Laura probably gave very little thought to her 50th anniversary, much less what she might wear on that occasion. Nonetheless, she is pictured here in 1911, 50 years and four children later, wearing her wedding gown.

Submitted by Elizabeth Rivers

Polish Immigrants ▶

Sarah Finkelstein is pictured with her two sons, Abe (center) and Henry, upon arriving in the United States from Kaluszyn, Poland in 1918. Sarah and Joe Finkelstein moved to Charleston in the early 1930s with their four children (two children were born in the United States) and established a grocery store on Huger Street. The family ran the business on the street level and lived above, on the second floor.

Submitted by Lorraine Finkelstein

Boxcar Explosion ▼

This photo, part of Julian Smith's collection now held by his daughter, depicts an unidentified man cleaning up after a boxcar explosion at the Ports Utilities, now called the State Ports Authority. The sides of the boxcars were splintered like matchsticks and part of the train was blown off the rails.

Submitted by Jacqueline Mappus

An Outing to the Battery ▼

Pictured here in February 1912 are Marie Welling (far right), her sister Emma and brother Edwin (in the back). The girls attended Memminger Normal School; Edwin later attended the High School of Charleston.

Submitted by Betty McMichael

SMS Charlotte ▲

The German sailing ship was docked in Charleston prior to World War I. German residents in Charleston entertained the sailors and in return, they were invited onboard the ship. Pictured here around 1910 are Jennie (Sindorf) Wieters, Irma (Sindorf) Young and Walter Frhr Von Lechordorf.

Submitted by Lisa L. Longshore

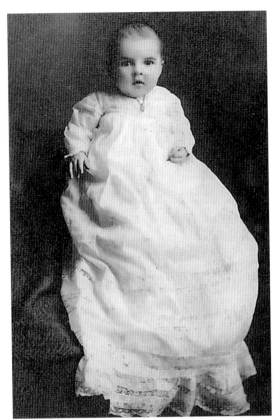

Avery Graduate ▶

Lucille Turner McCottry graduated from Avery Normal Institute on Bull Street in 1908. At Avery all girls learned cooking and sewing; they were required to make their own graduation dresses with the caveat that the price could not exceed $1. Lucille was an accomplished seamstress; she sewed at Belk and Kerrison's in the 1930s and '40s.

Submitted by Cynthia McCottry Smith

Wando Swimming Hole ▼

Best friends Ida Welling (left) and Emma Tharin enjoyed swimming in the Wando River down by the old sawmill in 1918. The girls went through school together and grew up in what is now called Cainhoy.

Submitted by Ruth Tharin Smith

Baptized in Faith ▲

And clothed in love and family history. The baptismal gown of Lucretia (Murphy) Nowak, worn in 1912 at St. Patrick's Church on St. Philip Street, is the same gown worn by Ashlyn Elizabeth Boudolf 82 years later at the Church of the Nativity on Folly Road. Lucretia Rowand Murphy made the gown of organza and embroidered lace. The bodice and upper sleeves are accented with satin ribbon. The gown is still lovingly kept by Ashlyn's grandfather, perhaps to be used at future family baptisms.

Submitted by Deborah Robinson Nelson

Practicing for the Pavilion ▲

These girls may have been practicing for a dance at the Isle of Palms Pavilion in 1914. The girls had been buddies for a number of years; they were all confirmed at the same time at St. Johannes Lutheran Church. Pictured from left to right: Edith (Momier) Strohmeyer, an unidentified girl, Elise C. (Patjens) Proctor, Lula (Steinberg) Harley.

Submitted by Elise Talbert

A Day in the Square ◄

Pictured at Citadel Square, now Marion Square, is George F. Wieters, Jr. and his nanny "Da" around 1917. The family lived at 99 Alexander St., not far from Marion Square.

Submitted by Lisa L. Longshore

Buggy Ride ▲

Emma Tharin, Ida Welling and an unidentified friend took a buggy ride down the main road in Wando in 1918. Parasols were standard issue for every occasion at that time, even a buggy ride to the store. The girls likely paid a visit to S.H. Venning Grocery Store pictured in the background.

Submitted by Allison McCarthy

Family Outing ▲

Eight family members are set to take the Franklin out for a drive in 1912. The family lived at 34 Smith St., a home Julius H. Jahnz purchased in 1902 for $10,000. The side of the home backed up to the Wentworth mansion; from her bedroom window Irma Jahnz could hear tennis games being played on the mansion court. Pictured in the car, back row left to right: Emily (Jahnz) Lesemann, Charlotte (Jahnz) Gaillard, Hulda (Jahnz) Cappelmann. Middle row: Julia (Jahnz) Roberts, Elsa (Jahnz) Schirmer. Emil Jahnz is in the driver's seat, next to Marie (Jahnz) Stender and Irma (Jahnz) Murray, with her doll. At the top of the stairs leading to the impressive entrance are Mr. and Mrs. Julius H. Jahnz and their son, Julius, Jr.

Submitted by Mary Lou Coombs

Bathing Beauties ◄

It was a common form of entertainment around 1916: families would take the ferry across to the Isle of Palms, catch the trolley and spend the day picnicking and swimming. These girls, all decked out in their swimming attire, lived in Mount Pleasant. On the far left is Margaret (Patjens) Eaton; the girl leaning over in the front is Eliese (Tiencken) Farmer. The little girl on the right is Laura (Patjens) Moye and the tallest young lady in the back is Elise C. (Patjens) Proctor.

Submitted by Elise Talbert

All in the Family ▶

John Andreas Patjens (back row, left), his brother Adolph (center back) and their sister Wilhelmina (Patjens) Tiencken (front right) are pictured with their spouses in 1913. John's wife Annie (Kruer) Patjens (front row, left), Adolph's wife Charlotte (Baum) Patjens and Wilhelmina's husband Herman Frederick Tiencken round out the brothers-and sisters-in-law. John ran the post office in Mount Pleasant; his brother Adolph ran Patjens Grocery Store on Church Street in Mount Pleasant. Brother-in-law Frederick Tiencken was also in the grocery business; his store was on Vanderhorst Street in Charleston.

Submitted by Elise Talbert

Gaud School

Watt School

Porter Military Academy

Porter-Gaud Class of 2008

Still making history after 140 years

PORTER GAUD

Since 1867

300 Albemarle Road
Charleston, SC 29407
(843)402-4775
PORTERGAUD.edu

1920s

Otranto Hunting Club

Sporting everything from firearms to bows and arrows and even slingshots, these gentlemen posing are ready for the hunt. Otranto Plantation is a subdivision now, but the home pictured in the background still exists. Edward Alexander Simons, on the far right, is the only man identified.

Submitted by Carlton Simons

Summer at Sullivan's ◄

Every summer this group of family and friends rented a house at Sullivan's Island. Pictured here in 1923 are (left to right): Lucille (Stemmermin) Johnson, Lucille (Pieper) Smith, Gertrude (Pieper) Johnston, Olivette (Pommer) Painter.

Submitted by Jacqueline Mappus

Adams Run Family ▼

Irene Dent and her brother Leroy had just returned home from Faith Presbyterian Church services in 1923 when this photo was taken. Their parents Alice Patsy (King) Dent and William Dent owned the property in the background.

Submitted by Lou Ethel and Helen Mitchell

Washington Park Memories ◄

Between Broad and Meeting streets is a tucked-away childhood play place that has changed very little over the last century. Mary Livingstain Sholk and the family's child care provider Julia often walked to the park for playtime.

Submitted by Susan Z. Hitt

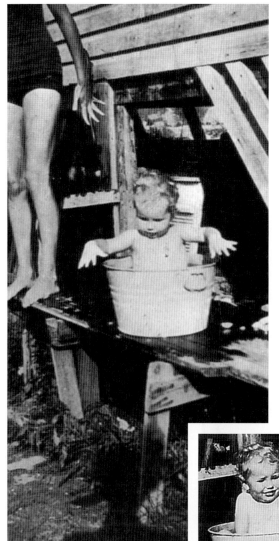

Taking a Break from the Bridge ▲

Billy Schleppergrill (left), Winton Surrat and
Marion Moore (right) took a breather from bridge
construction in the late 1920s. Moore finished Georgia
Tech in 1927 and married in 1928. The concrete bridge
spanning the Ashley River was a pleasing addition
to the Charleston landscape at its completion in the
mid-1930s.

Submitted by Jack Moore

The Baby and the Bath Water ◄

Little Barbara Melchers Traynor enjoyed her very
own makeshift kiddie pool in 1926. Although the
washboard behind her would seem to indicate she was
getting a good scrubbing, Barbara
was probably doing more soaking and
splashing. Her aunt Virginia Melchers,
standing on the left, probably would
have agreed.

*Submitted by
Barbara Melchers Traynor Pack*

Father and Son Outing ▲

William and Lily Melchers owned a home at Station
19, Sullivan's Island, and the grandchildren loved
playing on the huge rocks that were right next to the
house. Pictured here around 1928 are Leo M. Traynor,
Sr. and Leo M. Traynor, Jr.

Submitted by Barbara Melchers Traynor Pack

Blue Ribbon Honors ▶

The Cathedral of St. John the Baptist on Broad Street recognized its Grammar School honor students in 1929. Left to right: J. Fleming McManus, Aimar Brandt, Edward F. Conner, Jr., John F. Harrington, Jr.

From estate of the late Rev. Msgr. John Fleming McManus, submitted by Caroline Alexander

School Chums ▼

These young ladies were classmates at Memminger High School in 1924. At that time Memminger was a girls' school. Eighteen-year-old Clara Marie Rugheimer is pictured on the top row, far right.

Submitted by Sandy Campbell

Musical Mother and Son

Edna Peeples, a soprano who sang with the Charleston Choral Society and performed at venues in the mid-1920s, and her son Ralph Peeples, Sr. are pictured near Drake Street when Ralph was about 3 years old. Ralph would begin classical piano training at age 6; he grew up to play professionally at such well-known establishments as the Mills House and Cavallaro. Ralph was as an employee of the shipyard, but his life was his music.

Submitted by Martha Attisano

Life in the 1920s

Leon Joseph Oliver (left) was 27 years old in 1923, living with his family at 11 Pinckney St. He and his wife, Maggie Jackson Oliver, are pictured with 5-year-old Elisa (Oliver) Scrughan (in the back), 3-year-old Buddy and 10-month-old Stella (Oliver) Wilson, sitting on her father's knee.

Submitted by Donna Thomas

Patrolling the Border at the ▲ French Huguenot Church

Brothers Percy Allison Friend and Jimmy Friend are dressed in their uniforms, but the two men and James's wife Pearl are not patrolling the Mexican border on this day around 1919. They are pictured here in front of the French Huguenot Church, enjoying a leisurely afternoon. James and Pearl Friend lived on Spring Street and later on Oswego Street. The uniforms pictured were worn between 1917 and 1924 by the men who were assigned to patrol the Mexican border.

Submitted by Veronica Friend Wolfswinkel

May I Have This Dance? ◄

Julian Allen Smith and Lucille Catherine Pieper took advantage of the huge sandy dance floor at Sullivan's Island just before they married in 1925.

Submitted by Marilyn Weeks

Battery Athletic Club ▲

This group of boys ranging in age from mid-teens down to about 7 years old played basketball and baseball in the back yard of 29 Legare St. Those who could be identified in this photo, taken in December 1921, are: Angus Baker, Baron Holmes, David Dwight, Jr., Irvin Heyward, Strodwick Nash, Jr., Jack Wilbur, Tom Waring, "Bunky" Middleton, Charles Jervey, "Theo" Maybank, Sam Williams, Bill Gaud, Edgar Robertson, Joe Marshall, Tom Bennett, Harry Von Kolnitz, Francis Myers, Jr., "Sun" O'Neil, Ashmead Pringle, Jonnie Maybank, John Read, Keith Marshall, Henry Gaud, Wallace Jefferson, Hugh Nash, "Boots" Rhett, Harry Young and "Buster" Whaley.

Submitted by Mary Baker Pringle

American Legion Champs ▲

Post 112 won the state American Legion Baseball Championship in 1929. Back row (left to right): Johnny Douglas, Buddy Stehmeyer, Norman Welch, Bill Waugh, Gerald McMahon, Charles Ravenel, James Moseley, Danny Jones. First row: Eugene Eiserhardt, Tom Hutto, Gordon Doran, Gene Johnson, Ross Santos, Jake Hester, Buddy Witham.

Submitted by Jerry McMahon

Inauguration Day ▲

There was big excitement the day the Cooper River Bridge opened to two-way traffic Aug. 8, 1929. Downtown businesses closed and formal festivities were plentiful, including a parade across the new structure. Stationing for the parade probably took place in front of The Citadel on Marion Square, where 7-year-old Eleanor Rugheimer was waiting in the sidecar with several other young ladies to take part in the history-making event. The bridge, which was a toll road for a number of years, was later renamed the John P. Grace Memorial Bridge in honor of the Charleston mayor who helped make the connector between Mount Pleasant and Charleston a reality.

Submitted by Eleanor R. Pearce

Georgia Tech Students at Fort Moultrie, 1927 ▲

The men pictured were in the reserves in June 1927. By that time, Batteries Bingham, McCorkle and Jasper to the southeast would have been outfitted with rapid-fire guns as well as disappearing cannon capable of firing a 571-pound cannonball almost eight miles.

Submitted by Jack Moore

Bathing Beauty ◄

Lucille Catherine Pieper, pictured here in 1922, posed on a piling at Sullivan's Island in full bathing attire: hat, suit, socks and shoes, all of which were probably made of wool. The 1920s ushered in the first wave of form-fitting swimwear. Suits began to explore fabric colors beyond the traditional gray.

Submitted by Marilyn Weeks

Mary Street School Teachers

Mamie Turner (second from left), Miss Hern (third from left) and Lucia Brown (in front) are the only women who could be identified in this 1922 photo. Mary Street School was an elementary school. It is now the Shaw Center.

Submitted by Cynthia McCottry Smith

Beaux and Belles ▲

This young person's theatrical group performed in downtown Charleston as a part of a school function May 11, 1923. From left to right: William Burke with Mildred Collins, Marion Ducker with Louise Sanders, Dallas Kuhn, standing behind Herbert Lowry who is holding the placard, John Matthews with Doris Disher, Robert Knox with Mary Collins.

Submitted by Dallas Kuhn

Chief Cantwell, 1920 ▲

Chief of Police James R. Cantwell began his tenure as Chief of Police in 1920, serving under Mayor John P. Grace. Shown here at the family's home at 86 Cannon St. is Cantwell's wife Mary Ellen, and the youngest of their five children, Maree Cantwell Schwerin. When Cantwell died at the age of 63, Mayor Grace served as a pallbearer.

Submitted by Mary Ellen (Schwerin) Shorter

Sitting on the Dock of the Bay ◀

Or rather, the dock of the Carolina Yacht Club on East Bay Street. Shortly after the marriage of Arthur and Patience Middleton, the couple enjoyed a warm afternoon overlooking the water.

Submitted by Annely Klingensmith

Gibbes Art Gallery Pond

In the late 1920s Dorothy (Boots) Ott (left) and her mother Rosa (second from left) accompanied some friends to the Gibbes Art Gallery a block and a half from their home on Queen Street. "Boots" was given her nickname by an older brother because, when he came home and took his boots off, Dorothy would run and put them on. Her full nickname was "Boots Without Shoes," but evidence provided in this photo suggests that she did have her own pair. The lily pond has since been cemented over.

Submitted by Judy Chapman

Pieper and Pommer Families ▲

Jacqueline Smith (first row, third from left) and her father Julian (back row, second from left) were among the friends and family at Sullivan's Island in 1928.

Submitted by Jacqueline Mappus

Boating at the Pier ◀

Generally it is advisable to include water when boating, but the children didn't seem to miss it. These friends and family enjoyed a day trip to Folly in 1929, when there was no amusement park or arcade at the beach. Fun was where you found it, even in a beached boat. Pictured left to right are: Walter, Gertrude, Bill, and Genevieve Duane, and Logan Kornahrens on the far right. Behind him are Louis and Marguerite Boudolf, and Francis Oliver, back row on the left.

Submitted by Mary Coy

The Maguire Family

John M. Maguire and his family lived at 24 Wentworth St. in 1920, a block away from the fire station on the corner of Wentworth and Meeting streets. All three of Maguire's children were born in the house: Margaret, nicknamed "Marguerite" (left), Helen (right) and Catherine (second row, right). His wife Margaret "Maggie" (McLaughlin) Maguire is seated next to her husband on the left. The house had belonged to her parents, James J. and Catherine K. McLaughlin.

Submitted by Margie Walker Limbaker

A Bag of Bread and Birds ▲

Hampton Park was a magical place for children in the 1920s; with a bread sack, a child could be entertained for hours feeding the ducks, swans and geese that populated the pond. Pictured here on a cold day in 1921 are Elisabeth Wieters (left) and Wilma Young.

Submitted by Lisa L. Longshore

Walter on Wall

In 1926 little Walter Duane stood on Wall Street, facing south toward Minority Street. The spot where Walter stood to be photographed would become the site of the Gaillard Auditorium some 40 years later.

Submitted by Mary Coy

The Citadel, The Military College of SC ▲

This photo, taken shortly before The Citadel moved to its present location, depicts the Charleston skyline in the early 1900s.

Submitted by Elizabeth Rivers

Double Duty ▶

Frank H. Thames employed Rachel Nelson in 1929 as a nanny to twin boys Donald Watson Thames and Jack Conrad Thames. For 12 years Rachel went everywhere with them, assisting in the care of the boys' older brother Frank H. Thames, Jr. as well.

Submitted by Anne Thames

Maum "Bet" ▲

The children of Henry Fowles, Jr. and Evelyn (Hart) Rivers are pictured here in the arms of Rebecca Stoney in 1928. The family lived on Belvidere Plantation on Johns Island; their "maum," a commonly used term of respect, lived down the street. She is holding Henry F. Rivers (left) and Joseph L. Rivers.

Submitted by Joseph L. Rivers

Newlywed ▽

Ida (Schreiberg) Levin had been married about a year in this photo, taken in 1923. Her husband was stationed in Charleston with the U.S. Navy as a CPO Bandmaster. He performed numerous concerts at the Battery with the Navy Band.

Submitted by Mitzi L. Kirshtein

Holding Down the Copen ▲

In 1929 many homes had a decorative cement or brick enclosure around the house, which is remembered as a "copen." Evelyn Mims' whole family lived on Charlotte Street at that time; she enjoyed playing on the copen when she was growing up.

Submitted by Evelyn Mims

Engaging Couple ◄

When Sylvia Charen said "yes" to Max Hirsch in 1920, she could not have known that one day she would be married to Charleston's "Singing Milkman." When the Depression hit in 1932, work was hard to come by. Hirsch always enjoyed singing, entering any radio contests that came along. But the cream really came to the top when he put his talents to work delivering milk for Crescent Dairy on Meeting Street and later for Rephan Dairy. "The Singing Milkman" got up every morning at 3 a.m., regardless of the weather, because he knew school children were depending on him.

Submitted by Betty Hirsch Lancer

Schmidts at St. Philip Street ▼

Diedrich H. H. Schmidt, Sr. and his wife Nathalie E. Schmidt lived on St. Philip Street, down from the old police station, in the 1920s. The family later moved to Charlotte Street. All the windows in the house were open to encourage some sort of breeze; a laundry tub hangs below the downstairs window.

Submitted by Evelyn Mims

Football Back in the Day ▲

As a 19-year-old at the High School of Charleston in 1930, Johnny Robinson loved to play football for Coach Billy Bostwick. His positions included quarterback and halfback; he was team captain during his senior year. His athletic prowess earned him a football scholarship to Presbyterian College. In those days most cities had just one high school so teams traveled to play each other. Charleston's games were held at Johnson Hagood Stadium.

Submitted by Deborah Robinson Nelson

Construction of the Ashley River ▲ Memorial Bridge

The foundations of the Ashley River Bridge, part of the Atlantic Coast Highway system, were under construction in the 1920s. The bascule bridge (the French word for "seesaw") was a double-leaf drawbridge, opening in the middle and lifting to both sides. The bridge was dedicated in 1926.

Submitted by Jack Moore

1928 Sullivan's Island ▲ Rock-Climbing Champions

Children love climbing things, and the rocks beside William and Lily Melchers' second home at Station 19 were too irresistible to pass up. The conquest required a photo in the late '20s; pictured are Barbara, Leo and Caroline Traynor.

Submitted by Barbara Melchers Traynor Pack

Wall Street Declines ◄

In the 1920s Wall Street was a working class Irish neighborhood of Charleston single houses. Only a small part of Wall Street remains today; many of the homes were demolished for the Gaillard Auditorium, built in 1968. This photo shows Joe Duane, a machinist, with his wife Mattie (Murphy) and their son Bill at their home, 16 Wall St., on Christmas Day around 1922. Young Bill, one of nine Duane children, models the cowboy costume he received for Christmas: hat, lasso, and kerchief. Bill provided the hankerin' for adventure; he grew up to become a career Navy man as a chief and corpsman.

Submitted by Mary Coy

1930s

Paving SC 61 ▲

Edward E. Anderson, wearing overalls, a necktie and hat, was working for the county as chief mechanic in the mid-1930s when he prepared the roadbed for paving Highway 61. He drove the Caterpillar tractor from Columbia to Charleston to be used for the roadwork. At that time the equipment garage was somewhere in the vicinity of the intersection of Wappoo and Ashley River roads.

Submitted by Raymond Anderson

Easter at Edgewater ▲

Irma and Johnnie Murray enjoyed Easter Day in the 1930s at the home of Julius H. Jahnz. The home at 1411 South Edgewater Drive in Edgewater Park was considered to be one of the most beautiful suburban estates in Charleston at that time.

Submitted by John Coombs

Wedding Nuptials ▶

The wedding party of Clara Marie (Rugheimer) Simmons and Stephen E. Simmons gathered at the Rugheimers' home, 37 Montagu St., for their wedding luncheon April 29, 1930. Pictured left to right are: Charles E. Norton, Caroline Anderson, Steve Simmons (the groom), Charles Tamsberg, Clara Marie (Rugheimer) Simmons (the bride), John Peter Rugheimer, Johanna and John Peter Rugheimer (parents of the bride), and Erna Rugheimer.

Submitted by Sandy Campbell

Nothing But Chickens In Here

And some turkeys, geese, pigeons and guinea hens. The Hen House also sold groceries and meats at 646 King St. In 1939 Ted Mappus was only about 12 years old but he had two jobs: cutting the heads off chickens and making deliveries on his bicycle, parked out front.

Submitted by Ted Mappus

Courtenay Class Outing ▲

Henrietta Givner's Courtenay School 7th grade class took a field trip to Hampton Park in 1937. One of the park bridges is visible in the background on the right. Ms. Givner was an exceptional teacher, far ahead of her time, according to her students. Those that could be identified are: Edward Rourk, Doris Levy, Helene Firetag, Goldie Willis, Mary Godwin, Rosalie Livingston, Bob Mendez, Henry Thiele, Rose Givner, Clemmy Cox, Julia Oxler, Mary Fickling, Fannie Appel, Bessie Slotchiver, Emanuel Knight, Melvin Firetag, Mary Matson, Bernard Solomon, Bernie Novit and Francis Smith.

Submitted by Fannie Appel-Rones

The Wave ▼

Sarah King (left) and her friend, Mary Collette, nicknamed "Ting," lived on Yonges Island but often enjoyed socializing at Folly Beach. The girls attended St. Paul's High School and were about 17 years old at the time of this photo, in 1935.

Submitted by Nancy Smoak Peeples

Crafty Little First Graders ▲

These proud students represent the entire first grade at Craft School, at Legare and Queen streets, in 1938. Children lived nearby, close enough to take the "Ankle Express" to school each morning, as Bobby and Claudia Burdell's father liked to call it. Craft School is now condominiums.

Submitted by Claudia FitzGerald

Have Goat, Will Travel ▲

Some folks earned their living as traveling photographers in the early 1930s, taking pictures of children inside the photographer's goat-powered wagon. Janet (Garris) Meacher, 3 years old, had the opportunity to hitch a ride at her home at 96 Congress St. in 1932.

Submitted by Rembert Garris

Prize Fighter ▶

Woodrow "Newsboy" Beasley was a prize fighter in the 1930s. He earned his nickname because of his service with *The News and Courier* and *The Evening Post*. He boxed in 98 fights, winning 89 of them. Additionally, he coached Golden Gloves in the '40s as well as the newspaper's amateur boxing team. He is pictured here in 1933 on his Harley-Davidson motorcycle.

Submitted by John Beasley

ST. ANDREW'S LUTHERN CHURCH - 1936 CONFIRMATION

St. Andrew's Lutheran Confirmation Class ◄

In 1936 Della Caroline Stebner (front row, third from right) and Benton Theiling Stebner (back row, fourth from left) were confirmed at their parents' church on Wentworth Street. Pastor Charles Felch officiated. The Stebner family lived on Anson Street "in the borough." The children grew up watching the old men make crab and fish nets on Adgers Wharf.

Submitted by Benita Stebner Kinlaw

Family Fun at Folly ▶

Louie Martens, Otto Martens, Aline Martens (in the back), Betty Kangeter and Rosie Martens (right) always enjoyed day trips to Folly in the summer. In the late 1930s Folly Beach was Charleston's version of Coney Island, with a pier and pavilion and four "thrill" rides including swings and a merry-go-round. The Martens children, and cousin Betty from New York, spent many entertaining hours playing in the surf and running back to their "tent" on the beach. Since cars were allowed to drive on the beach at that time, adults commonly lifted the trunk and spread out blankets—instant shelter from the sun.

Submitted by Rose Bolchoz

South Battery Backyard ▲

E. DuBose Blakeney, III and his mother, Frances Bissell Blakeney, were photographed in 1939 on the joggling board in the backyard of 32 South Battery, his great-aunt's home.

Submitted by E. DuBose Blakeney, III

Barefoot Buddies ▲

Gary Early (left) and Malcolm
Crosland were neighbors on
Tradd Street during their youth.
The boys enjoyed running
around shoeless in Charleston
in the summer. Early said it was
too hot and they couldn't afford
them anyway.

Submitted by Gary Early

Out-of-Town Relatives ▲

The Montgomery and Snider families from Kingstree, S.C., came to Charleston by
train to visit family around 1932. Everyone toured the sites, including a visit by ferry
to Isle of Palms. The relatives had their picture taken in front of the Isle of Palms Bath
House. Edward Rush Montgomery is third from the right wearing a dark tie.

Submitted by Betty Rosen

Charleston Piazzas and Petals ◄

Robert E. Couturier helped his mother in her garden at 13 Bogard St. He was about
25 years old in this photo, taken Oct. 23, 1934. His daughter's nickname, "Tuney,"
sprang from this very spot. Someone once remarked that Mrs. Couturier grew lovely
petunias in her garden; she replied that her granddaughter, Celeste, was her nicest
petunia. Celeste was known, from then on, as "Tuney."

Submitted by Celeste Cornell

Charleston County Police Force ▽

Rudolph W. Knight, Sr. served 37 years with the department, in uniform as well as many years as a detective. Pictured here in 1937 (first row, left to right): Cox, Santos, Nelson, Bearings, Costa. Second row: Morseman, Herron, Leland, Wilkerson, Middleton. Third row: Rudolph W. Knight, Sr., Simmons, Henderson, Ivey, Young. Standing: Limbaker.

Submitted by Annie S. Knight

Home From the Pet Parade ▲

Eugene Fox took his nephews Leroy Gissell (left) and Robert Gissell to the High Battery for the Azalea Festival's Pet Parade around 1936. To take part in the parade the boys had to produce a pet, so they borrowed a biddie from their father, who raised chickens in the backyard, and put it in a bird cage. The boys' mother dressed them in overalls to look like farmers. Fox worked his entire life at *The News and Courier* as a linotype operator, making and setting type with molten lead poured into molds. Leroy retired from the Charleston Navy Yard; Robert retired from Lockheed Martin after 34 years at the Polaris Missile Facility Atlantic in Goose Creek.

Submitted by Robert Gissell

Miss Sally Carew's School ◄

Miss Sally Carew taught kindergarten and first grade to small groups of children in 1933 at 11 Orange St. The main house had a building in the back which was used as a private school. Annely Middleton is pictured on the far left; her sister Sally is on the far right.

Submitted by Annely Klingensmith

Medical College of S.C. School of Nursing ▼

Pictured in the 1932 graduating class is Edith (Montgomery) Knight who became a head nurse at the original Roper Hospital after her graduation. She is standing on the third row, second from left.

Submitted by Annie S. Knight

Civilian Conservation Corps ▲

Walter L. Seyle, Jr., pictured in the required dress for the CCC, worked two years building roads. The Civilian Conservation Corps was a government program that created jobs during the Great Depression. He was 22 years old in 1935.

Submitted by Lisa Kynoski

Family Fun at Folly ▲

D.H.H. Schmidt, Nathalie Emily Schmidt, Evelyn
Jeanette McGee, Johnny Rourk, Mazie Rourk Schmidt
and "Dick" Schmidt took a drive on the beach in the
early 1930s. Uncle Dick, on the far right, apparently was
the self-appointed inner tube monitor that day.

Submitted by Evelyn Mims

Ferry to North Island ▲

Doris Maher's father James was in the lighthouse
service in the late 1930s; the only way over to the
lighthouse at North Island was by ferry. And the only
way to get across by ferry was to be pulled on a cable.
The man on the left with his foot braced against a
board is rowing the ferry across to the island. Doris is
standing; her mother Kate is seated on the lighthouse
service truck.

Submitted by Doris Maher Richards

Little Drummer Boy ▶

Jackie Flemming, grandson of Mr. and Mrs. J. F. Brenner,
Sr., looks like he was practicing for future membership
in the Drum and Bugle Corps in August 1934. Jackie's
grandparents lived at 6 Court House Square.

Submitted by Annie S. Knight

Flower Power ▲

The Ladies Auxiliary Charleston City Fire Department float was ready to roll in 1930, with Monica (Grooms) Garris (far right) behind the wheel. The Azalea Festival Parade was always a big Charleston event. Mrs. Garris was the wife of Second Assistant Fire Chief Edward Thomas Garris. The photo was taken at Wentworth and Meeting streets.

Submitted by Rembert Garris

Hampton Park Hat Exchange ▶

It was customary in 1939 for both men and women to wear a hat just about everywhere, but generally men wore men's hats, and ladies wore ladies' hats. This photo, taken on a Sunday afternoon visit to Hampton Park with friends just prior to their marriage, Louis Henry Sohl and Mattie (Brown) Sohl decided to exchange accessories. The couple were married more than 60 years.

Submitted by Carl Sohl

Bishop England Graduate ▲

Lucretia Murphy graduated from Bishop England High School in 1930. She is pictured here, all smiles, at her aunt's home, 70 Smith St. The home is still a residence.

Submitted by Chet Nowak

Mitchell Mites ▲

During the 1930s the city of Charleston employed Corrine Jones and her son Danny to establish and promote park and playground activities for children. Mitchell, Hampton and Moultrie parks were a few of the parks established at that time, promoting wholesome activities and healthy lifestyles. The Mitchell Mites baseball team of 1937 was just one of many groups of young people who benefited from the Jones' efforts. Pictured (front row, left to right): L. Cuzzell, A. Whitter, W. Shiver, O. Myers, J. Albers, M. Costa. Back row: H. Able, C. McDaniel, L.A. Sires, "Foxy" Petit (coach), C.D. Petit, J. Duc, C. Weeks. Not pictured: L. Scott, E. Vonderleith, L. Brown.

Submitted by LeRoy Sires

Blue Ribbon Recipients ▲

Courtenay School, corner of Meeting and Mary streets, awarded blue ribbons in the 1930s to all first graders who passed certain tests and maintained good health during the school year. Vivian (Blackmon) Skelton (front row, third from right) was one of those proud pupils. The original Courtenay School was later torn down and a new school was built in its place.

Submitted by Vivian Skelton

Four Dorothys ◄

In the mid-1930s these four first cousins, all named Dorothy, had their photo taken on the Battery. Pictured left to right: Dorothy Solomon Sherman, Dorothy Goldberg Berger, Dorothy Rosen Cohen, Dorothy Gelson Cohen.

Submitted by Sydney Richman

Crepe Paper Car ▲

On special occasions such as the Schützenfest, the Stehmeiers decorated their car from stem to stern. It must have taken hours to cover the car, and even longer to uncover it, but the effort was certainly worth it. Pictured on Marion Square in 1937 to the right of the car are: Frances Tollener, Herman Stehmeier, his son Herman William Stehmeier, and his wife Martha Stehmeier.

Submitted by Herman Stehmeier

Hollis & Hollis Garage ▲

Clyde Walters (second from the left) was in his early 30s when he worked at the garage on Cannon Street. He had gone to Detroit Diesel School and knew all about cars. He knew how to blend business with pleasure too; he used to wear his "dating clothes" underneath his coveralls when he courted his girlfriend Lucille Prine. The couple were married in 1932.

Submitted by Elizabeth Thomas

Great-Grandmother Oliver ◄

Elisa (Montenese) Oliver's father had come to America from Spain, and made his home in Charleston. She and her husband Leon Joseph Oliver had 10 children; she is pictured here in the 1930s, probably at their home on Pinckney Street.

Submitted by Donna Thomas

Blue Ribbon Babies ▲

These 6-year-olds at Craft School have all been vaccinated, and have earned their Blue Ribbons for health. The 1930 photo was taken at a doctor's home on Murray Boulevard. Those who could be identified include: Gerard Stelling, Kenneth Marvin, Cambridge Trott, Frances Jenkins, Anne Johnson, Mary Bargman, Jean Matthews, Betty Wilbur, Frederica Readen, Dorothy Dixen, William Ostendorff, Harry Trapolis, Constance Lempesis, Dougal Bissell, Eleanor Canfield, Charlie Passerella, Carl Poleanon, Mack Lyons, Louis Stender.

Submitted by Anne Allison

The Hen House Boys ◄

Ted Mappus (left), age 10, and his brother James, age 6, lived at 646 King St. in 1936, where their father, T.T. Mappus, Sr., owned The Hen House. The boys attended Mitchell School but in the summertime, they helped out in the store.

Submitted by Ted Mappus

Puppy Play ◄

Herbie (left) and his twin brother Albie Wilcox lived next door to Josie Hofling and her brother Charlie on Cannon Street. When the Hoflings' water spaniel had a big litter in 1933, the boys kept the puppies entertained. And vice versa.

Submitted by Herbie Wilcox

Rifle Club Parade

It took Daisy Missel (left) all day to decorate for the parade, including making crepe paper flowers to adorn the floats. It took her husband, Charlie, just one afternoon of sharp shooting to adorn his jacket with medals won during the day's shooting events. The parade was held at Ashley Park, now the Rifle Club on Heriot Street. Margaret, Gloria, Walter and Charlie Missel are also pictured.

Submitted by Margaret Wilkes

Boy Scout Troop Seven

This fine group of young men met at the Cathedral of St. John the Baptist on Broad Street. It was the first Catholic Boy Scout troop in the city. Pastor Rev. James J. May is pictured in the center with the boys and troop leader John Edward (Eddie) Maher (seated third row, right.) The young man behind the drum in the white shirt is Sherman Willis. Sporting the uniform of the time, short pants and knee socks, neckerchiefs and Smokey the Bear hats, their slogan was to "Do a Good Turn Daily."

Submitted by Anne Comar Willis

Lifelong Friends ▶

Russell DuPuis (left) and his friend Herman Stramm grew up together on Cypress Street, riding their bikes all over Charleston County. The houses haven't changed much in 50 years, and neither has the relationship between these two friends.

Submitted by Herman Stramm

Self-Made Man ▶

Theodore A. Brown was 19 years old in 1936. Eight years later he opened Brown's Roofing and Sheet Metal Works, building his business by word of mouth. He retired in 1985 and the business he founded still thrives under his son's ownership.

Submitted by Maxine Poindexter

Servicing the Lighthouse ▼

James Maher was an inspector in the lighthouse service between 1935 and 1940. To get to the North Island lighthouse, you had to go by ferry. One car at a time would fit; the rowboat on the side was the only way for the men pulling the ferry to come and go. The mosquitoes were so thick on North Island that Maher's khaki pants looked gray within minutes of arrival.

Submitted by Doris Maher Richards

A Day at the Park ▲

Hampton Park was a lovely place to run around in 1938, especially around the duck pond. Joan Haught (right) was about 4 years old. She is pictured with her cousin Johnny Duane, about 3 at the time, and Joan's aunt Gertrude (Duane) Clark at the far right.

Submitted by Mary Coy

Flights of Fancy ▲

Aviation was relatively new in the early 1930s when Miss Susie Robinson's first-grade class took on the project of building "The Good Ship Lollipop." The Bennett School students used cardboard and paper to construct the airplane, and adorned their backdrop, entitled "The Lollipop Landing Field," with all manner of flying objects. They also included a hangar on the right, and a light tower in the back. Bennett School was located on the corner of George and St. Philip streets. It is now part of the College of Charleston.

Submitted by Elizabeth Rivers

First Day of School ◄

There appears to be a slight look of uncertainty on James Gary Early's face as he steps out of his home at 151 Tradd St. for his first day of school. Gary is the son of Horace Early, who ran the High School of Charleston's English Department for 22 years.

Submitted by Gary Early

1940s

RADIO JOINS THE FIGHT
AGAINST TB
1340
ON YOUR DIAL **WHAN** 1340
ON YOUR DIAL

The Fight Against TB

By the 1940s tuberculosis was finally curable for the first time with the development of effective anti-tubercular drugs. Locally, the fight against TB was supported with a special parade down King Street. WHAN Radio, owned by Harry Weaver, sponsored a car in the parade. Pictured in the back of the car (left to right): Trudy (Murphy) Moore, Bill Morgan, Carol Ballantine. The driver's name was Vernon.

Submitted by Deborah Robinson Nelson

Business School Buddies ▼

Bee (Means) Hutson (left), Jane (Lucas) Thornhill and Mavis (Perry) Barrett took time off from typing class at Rice Business School to visit Hampton Park in 1946. Part of the park's attraction for young women may well have been its proximity to The Citadel.

Submitted by Mavis Barrett

Fishing Off the Dock

Eugene DuBose Blakeney, III lived on Tradd Street just a few blocks from the Fort Sumter Hotel in 1945. During the summer months, when he wasn't attending Craft School, he enjoyed throwing a line in the water off the Fort Sumter Hotel dock. In this photo he is wearing his lucky fishing hat—the Navy cap worn by his uncle when he was in the service.

Submitted by E. DuBose Blakeney, III

Memminger Auditorium, Prior To Renovations ▼

This 1948 photo was taken in the school's auditorium, which was renovated and re-opened in 2008 for Spoleto Festival USA. These girls were the last all-girls' class to graduate from Memminger High School in 1950. Pictured on the far left: Rose (Martens) Bolchoz, Toula Latto, Coach Nancy McIver, Joanie (Dixon) Wilcox and Barbara Marino. The only other girl who could be identified is on the far right: Betty Lesseman.

Submitted by Rose Bolchoz

A Petit Christmas ▲

Linda (left) and Ann Petit display their Christmas gifts—stuffed animals and baby dolls—in their grandmother's back yard at 23 Cleveland St. in 1944. Linda was about a year old at the time; her sister was 3.

Submitted by Ann Bradt

Ladson Baptist Church ▲

The entire congregation is pictured in 1949, at the church's homecoming and picnic. Ladson Baptist was the first church built in Ladson; it has moved down Ladson Road toward the intersection of Highway 78 from its original location near the railroad crossing on Ladson Road.

Submitted by Mazie Brown

Home From the War ▶

John (left) and his brother Donald Leitch were on leave from World War II in the 1940s when this photo was taken with their sister Elizabeth. The boys were visiting relatives on Cleveland Street near Hampton Park.

Submitted by Ann Bradt

Pop Keller's Drive Inn ▲

Keller's was a great place for kids to hang out in 1943. Located on the Dual Lane Highway (now Rivers Avenue) in North Charleston, Keller's Drive Inn featured famous onion rings and barbecue sandwiches in addition to hamburgers, fried chicken and shrimp. There was a jukebox and dance floor, pinball machines and soda fountain. Pop Keller opened the establishment after World War II, offering dine-in or curbside service.

Submitted by Susie Childress

McLaughlin Wedding ▲

The marriage of Mary Clary Whiteside to William T. McLaughlin in 1941 was held at the Cathedral of St. John the Baptist on Broad Street. Both graduated from Bishop England High School and the College of Charleston. Mr. McLaughlin spent his career on Broad Street as a property and casualty insurance broker. Mrs. McLaughlin earned her master's degree in music from Columbia University in New York. She was a pianist and taught music at Bishop England and at Rivers High School.

Submitted by Tom McLaughlin

Closer to the Sun ▶

Delores Newman (left) and her friend Ruth Reeves climbed to the roof top of a 3 ½-story house on Smith Street to get a suntan one afternoon in 1946. Apparently someone with a camera thought of the idea before the girls did. Delores and Ruth were seniors at Memminger School at that time.

Submitted by Ruth Clark

Balancing Act ▲

Lawrence Moore, a member of the Shamrock Hand-Balancing Team, displays amazing strength as he lifts Rembert Garris overhead with one arm. Garris estimated his weight at 175 lbs. in 1949. The team worked out on Folly Beach by the old pier. The Pavilion is in the background.

Submitted by Rembert Garris

Tap Dance Revue ▶

Five-year-old Richard Goehring, Jr. (back row, center) wasn't too keen on tap dancing in the late 1940s, but he stuck it out for a year at Joan Simmons' Dance School on Wentworth. His cousin Jay Rumph (first row, second from left) took to tapping, however, eventually becoming an instructor. Tap lessons cost $5 per month for each boy; lessons were weekly. The boys wore one-piece outfits of purple velvet pants and fuchsia silk shirts with purple velvet hats to match.

Submitted by Richard Goehring, Jr.

Moore Store, Jedburg ▲

Reed and Margie Moore owned a Sinclair Gas Station at the crossroads of Jedburg on Highway 78 in the late 1940s and early '50s. The store sold everything: dry goods, clothing, groceries, farm supplies. The family lived behind the store in the house pictured. A new medical center occupies the property today.

Submitted by Annette Stack

Charleston Bar Bell Club, 1947 ▲

Most of the old YMCA's 25 members of the Bar Bell Club had been in the military, serving in World War II. When the war ended, the men enjoyed competing in body building and weight lifting in Charleston and Greenville. Of the 11 men pictured, only three can be identified: Lawrence Moore (left), Julian Clark (second from left) and Rembert Garris (far right, with lion tattoo).

Submitted by Rembert Garris

Ebenezer A.M.E. Sunday School ◄

The Sunday School class had their photo taken on the steps of Ebenezer A.M.E. Church, 44 Nassau St. in 1947. The church is still there; it has been remodeled and a fellowship hall has been added. Back row (left to right): Sunday School Superintendent Mr. Kinlaw, Janie Williams, teacher, Tom Brown, assistant superintendent, Loretta Young, teacher, Mrs. Hutchinson and Rev. B.J. Hutchinson. Students who could be identified include: Charlesetta Rivers, Angel Palmer, Margaret McLaughlin, Rebecca Green, Marilyn Steplight, Barbara Williams, Leroy Mowell, Rosalyn Benton, Penzola Williams. Gloria Williams.

Submitted by Debra P. (Angel) Green

Founder of Bishop England High School ▶

The first rector and founder of Bishop England High School, Rev. Joseph L. O'Brien, stands outside the Cathedral of St. John the Baptist on Broad Street, where graduation ceremonies were held for approximately 50 students in 1945. This was the school's 30th year in existence; founded as the Catholic High School in 1915, the school moved to Calhoun Street in 1916 and was renamed for Bishop John England, the first bishop of the Diocese of Charleston. The land is now the College of Charleston library; Bishop England relocated to Daniel Island.

Submitted by Anne Kingsley

District Intelligence Office, 1943 ▲

The DIO-6th Naval District was the Navy's intelligence arm, investigating sabotage and espionage. Their offices were located at 29 East Bay St. The building became a private residence after the war and remains so today. Pictured on the front row: Archie L. Harman, Marvin E. Luther, Walter S. Holman, William A. Gamble, George F. Ulmer, Cmdr. J. Lloyd Abbot, Lt. (jg) J.L. Wiggins, G. Truett Hucks, Morgan Arant, Frank S. Hull, and Wm. L. Hall. Back Row: Jesse R. Lowe, Roy L. Grant, Richard E. Page, John A. Pearson, William J. Snelling, Charles E. Snoddy, Franklin K. Odom, Raymond J. Zetell, Silas B. Knight, Wm. P. Tennent.

Submitted by J. Howard Hucks

Folly Frolicking ▲

It was not an unusual event for friends to get in a car and drive to, and on, Folly Beach in the late 1940s. Pictured here in 1948 (left to right) are: Charlean Crain, Chuck Kesson (he owned the car), Martha Crain, Jim Hutson, Barbara Hutson.

Submitted by Barbara Hudson

Malanos Wedding ◄

Emmanuel George Malanos was a Greek immigrant who served in the Greek Navy and then as a merchant seaman. In 1945, at age 30, he married Koula Bazakas, age 17, at the Greek Orthodox Church of the Holy Trinity on St. Philip Street (the site of the Crosstown now). A reception followed at the Bazakas home, 1202 King St. The couple were in the grocery business but later Mrs. Malanos opened a florist shop on Magnolia Road.

Submitted by Koula Malanos

Individual Swimming Pools ▲

Rudy Knight, age 4, and his sister Martha, age 6, find a satisfying solution to the July heat in 1946: personal pans of water. Rudy made sure he had the garden hose available for a constant flow of water in his tub. The family lived at 805 Montague Ave. in North Charleston. The building was sold in the 1960s to St. Thomas Episcopal Church next door.

Submitted by Annie S. Knight

Army-Navy Headquarters Building ▲

The District Intelligence Personnel-6ND-are pictured here in White Point Gardens, 1944. Their headquarters was in the old Fort Sumter Hotel, which later became offices and condominiums.

Submitted by J. Howard Hucks

Charleston Rinky Dinks ◄

The boys chose the team name "Rinky Dinks" from a cartoon by the same name in the 1930s. None of them turned out to be rinky dink players however; their 1948 season for the City YMCA League netted them the championship. Pictured is Harold Haynie, the team's center, on the left. Jim Runey with the Knights of Columbus team, is on the right.

Submitted by Robert Manning

Get On, and Pedal Fast

Nine-year-old Joyce M. LaFourcade taught her nephew Russell Willard Seyle, age 6, to ride a bike at the Seyles' home on Cannon Street in 1940. The boy's father worked at the State Utilities Railroad Commission until he retired after 51 years. The home at 157 ½ Cannon St. is now a parking garage.

Submitted by Lisa Kynoski

BE Returning Lettermen

1944 was the first year Bishop England had a football team. Pictured here are the returning lettermen for the 1945 season. Left to right: Dick Condon, Robbie Cole, Emmett Santos, John LaTorre, Furman Wham, Claude Blanchard.

Submitted by Jerry McMahon

Christmas Without the Flash

In 1946 if your camera didn't have a flashbulb, you had two options: flood the living room with lights, or drag the Christmas tree outside in the sunshine. Johnny Robinson, Jr. is pictured riding his scooter near the Christmas tree in his grandmother's backyard, 775 Rutledge Ave.

Submitted by Deborah Robinson Nelson

"Since 1840-Quality That Never Varies"

Carolina Beverage Sales' Studebaker delivery trucks were loaded with cartons of beer, ready to leave the business at 100 East Bay St. in the early '40s. The business distributed Genesee, Pilsener, Trim Beer and Carling's Red Cap Ale, according to the sign on the building. June (Reeves) Wireman (center) worked for the company after graduating from Memminger High School. Her twin, Jack Reeves, worked there as well. He is pictured on the far right. The man in front of the door is Tommy Lightsey, the owner. The business no longer exists.

Submitted by Anna Wireman McAllister

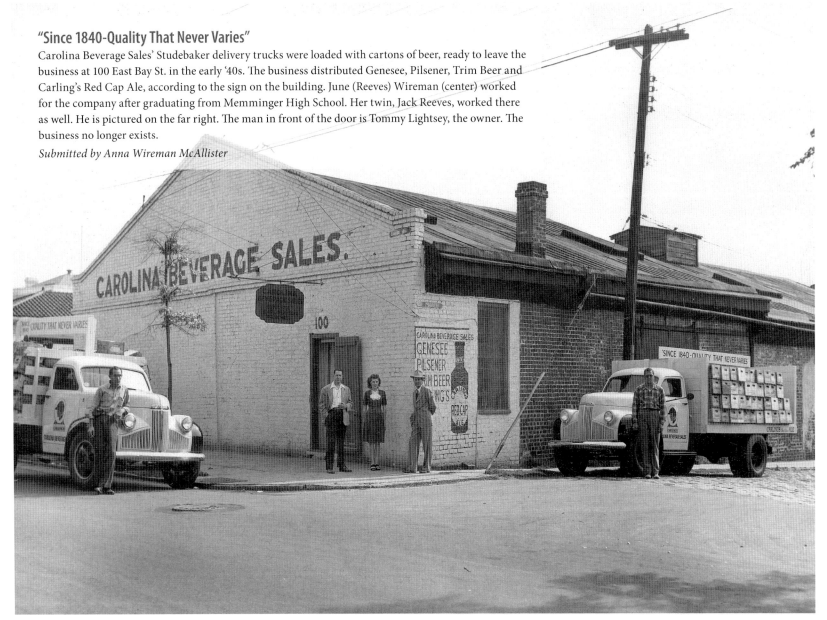

Toogoodoo Canoeing ◄

Preston King and his family took a boat trip on the Toogoodoo River on Yonges Island around 1940. The tiny boat appears to be carrying its maximum occupancy.

Submitted by Nancy Smoak Peeples

Four Generations of Murphys ►

George P.L. Murphy, Jr. (left) and his wife Lucretia Rowand Murphy (right) enjoy an afternoon on the porch of 71 Charlotte St. with their new son Patrick (George P.L. Murphy, III), pictured in the arms of Mrs. Murphy's mother, Bridget Byrne Rowand. The year was 1940. George and Lucretia Murphy built the house around 1915 and lived there, with their children and Lucretia's mother, for just one more year after this photo was taken. In 1941 the federal government purchased the home to build a post office, but it was never built. In 1963 the L. Mendel Rivers Federal Building was built with a parking lot in the rear. The house once stood on the same spot where the parking lot is now.

Submitted by Deborah Robinson Nelson

Little Gypsy Girl ▲

Ann Petit was dressed up as a gypsy at the home of Lizzy Leitch at 23 Cleveland St. Cleveland runs right into Hampton Park, where Ann loved to play when she wasn't in the backyard.

Submitted by Linda Lassiter

Legerton's 60th Anniversary ▲

In 1948 Legerton and Co. had a large business in office supplies, greeting cards, books and stationery at 263 King St. This was the store's second location; originally C.L. Legerton had his book and stationery store at 282 King. Employees who could be identified (left to right) are: Clifford Legerton, Jackie Truesdale, Gena Wilson, Frances Johnson, Felix Brockmann, Margretta Gaines, Ruth Hall, Merrile Martin, Alice Madden, C.L. Lyon, Mary Drescher. Not pictured are Betty Burnett and Ola C. Verdier.

Submitted by Merrile M. Kinard

Growing Up On The Groins ▲

Ray Schrecker (left), buddies Bobbie and Betty, and Bernie Schrecker (right) had a ready-made fort for childhood play on Folly in 1943. The Folly groins, and World War II barriers, on the right, were ideal for any number of uses, including picture-taking. The old Atlantic House is on the left in the background.

Submitted by Burnetta Schrecker

Festival Royalty ▲

As part of each year's May Day celebration, the crowning of the Festival King and Queen and installation of their court took center stage. The Community Building, located in front of Liberty Homes Graded School, was the backdrop in the early 1940s. Liberty Homes was a North Charleston neighborhood of hard-working people, most of whom were employed at the Naval Shipyard.

Submitted by Jan Perkins

Proud Parents ▶

Sol and Annie Rosen were proud of their son Morris who was in the Coast Guard from 1942–45. After the war he returned to law school at the University of South Carolina. He is still practicing law in Charleston today. The photo was taken at Mrs. Rosen's brother's home in Palmetto Gardens, North Charleston.

Submitted by Betty Rosen

The South's Oldest Daily Newspaper

In a city that values ancestry and tradition, The Post and Courier is the proud descendant of four newspapers: The Charleston Courier, The Charleston Daily News, The News and Courier and The Evening Post.

For the past 205 years, The Post and Courier and its predecessors have provided an unbroken record of service and history to its readers and the community. Through war, siege, fire, financial ruin, earthquakes and hurricane disaster, The Post and Courier's deep roots held strong.

Today, The Post and Courier's roots have grown even deeper into your community offering the coverage most convenient to you and your family.

The Post and Courier

BECAUSE KNOWING MAKES A DIFFERENCE.

The Evening Post   The News and Courier   The Charleston Daily News   The Charleston Courier

1894   1873   1865   1803

Son of Confederate Veteran ▲

Samuel Hampton Venning, pictured with his dog in the 1940s, was the son of a Confederate veteran. He ran Venning Store in Cainhoy, a business established in 1866 by his father, William Capers Venning, a lieutenant in Butler's Cavalry.

Submitted by Tharin Williamson

Teenage Memories ▲

This group of girls was visiting their friend Shirley Glaus (not pictured) in the early '40s. Shirley's family had a summer home at Folly on Front Beach. The girls spent the day walking and taking photos. Left to right: Lenora Webb, Joanie Wilcox, Lois Owen, Rosie Martens, Ruthie Robertson, Evelyn Ward.

Submitted by Joan Wilcox

Ready for the Beach ◄

Mary Schrecker, 27, is perched atop one of the old groins at Folly Beach in 1942. Mary and her husband lived in the 400-block on Folly with their three children for several years.

Submitted by Burnetta Schrecker

Knit For the Brits ▲

Every Friday afternoon this group of girls met at "Aunt Gertie" Bahr's home on Grove Street to knit for Britain in the 1940s. Aunt Gertie and her friend Cile West taught the girls to knit: first, squares for afghans, then scarves and sweaters, to be sent to servicemen overseas. Aunt Gertie provided the uniforms and caps with the Red Cross emblem on them.

Submitted by Joan Wilcox

Ladson Railroad Depot ◄

In 1940 a major mode of transportation was by rail; at that time Ladson had a depot with a shed and some benches for passengers coming and going. Alice Taylor (center) is the oldest daughter of Lile Adams, who ran a 13-room boarding house down the street. Wanda (left) and Bennie Taylor are pictured with their mother.

Submitted by Mazie Brown

Presentation of Debutantes ▲

The Gamma Xi Omega Chapter of Alpha Kappa Sorority, Inc. presented its first group of debutantes in 1949. Fathers presented their daughters at a ball held at the Charleston Air Base.

Submitted by Cynthia McCottry Smith

Red Cross Nurses' Aids ▶

Betty (Doscher) Mullen (left), Frances (Veralla) Masters and Doris (Puckhaber) Skuhra were single girls at the time this photo was taken, with regular jobs. But they chose to attend evening classes to become nurses' aids during World War II. They volunteered their services at Baker Hospital across from Colonial Lake on Ashley Avenue.

Submitted by Doris Skuhra

Memminger Reunion ◄

It was the first reunion of the last graduating class to finish their education in Memminger High School. Approximately 125 girls attended the event at The Colony House Restaurant.

Submitted by Norma Williams

Cold Weather Sailor ▼

Joseph I. Williams, Jr. was stationed in the North Atlantic in the mid 1940s; he is pictured here in his winter Navy uniform during World War II.

Submitted by Joe Williams

Third-Generation Charlestonian ▶

Walter W. Momeier, Jr. was a graduate of the High School of Charleston and The Citadel. He had been out of college for two years at the time of this photo, working as an accountant at Edward's Department Stores. He eventually became comptroller of the chain; he retired as finance director for the city of Charleston. He subscribed to both *The News and Courier* and *The Evening Post.*

Submitted by Greta Waters

Mirror Image ▽

At 13 years of age, Pat Murdaugh almost reflects the graceful beauty of the swan at Hampton Park in 1948. The family lived in Ashepoo, S.C. between Charleston and Walterboro.

Submitted by Pat Chassereau

First Grade, Synagogue Emanu-El ▲

These children attended school at Emanu-El when it was located on Gordon Street in 1948. Those who could be identified include: Eddie Toporek, Neil Draisin, Eliot Rabin, Nicky Bluestein, Ira Solomon, Ronnie Addlestone. The synagogue is now in West Ashley.

Submitted by Eileen Sorota

Last Class with 11 Years of School ▲

The Memminger High School class of 1947 was the last group to complete their education in 11 years. The girls were required to have the same number of credits as 12-year programs. Shown here in 1946 on the school grounds are (left to right): Betty Justice, Gertrude Frampton, Carolyn Neese, Dolores Hicks, Doris Carullo, Jean Hall, Grace Weeks.

Submitted by Dolores Manning

Home Away From Home ▼

USO Clubs provided recreation and a "home away from home" for enlisted men and women in the early 1940s. Dances were frequently held; some young men and women who met at the USO fell in love and married each other. Helen (Weil) Patla is the only person who could be identified; she is standing in the back next to a tall woman in front of the window.

Submitted by Alice Weil

8 North Hampstead

Pictured on July 3, 1940 are (left to right): Theresa Manning, Dave Low, Tally Tillman (former Charleston Police Chief), Harold Haynie, Tommie Manning. The black-and-white dog was named Snookie and belonged to Harold; the brown bulldog was Dixie.

Submitted by Robert Manning

Just Hangin' Out ▷

Some things never change, and a boy's love for cars is one of them. Richard Brewer was 18 years old in 1946 and a student at North Charleston High School. He is pictured here in the main business district of North Charleston, around Montague Avenue.

Submitted by Mary Brewer

Miller's Drug Store ▼
Geraldine (Mitchum) Guerry was employed at Miller's on Reynolds Avenue. She married one of the "Drug Store Cowboys." She began her employment at Miller's as a soda jerk, eventually working her way up to cosmetics.

Submitted by Geraldine Guerry

The Willard Bolchoz Swingers at the Cavallaro ▲
The Cavallaro on Highway 17 was the place to go in the late 1940s. Billed as "The South's Finest and Most Modern Dining and Dance Club," the Cavallaro provided "entertainment for your pleasure" and was "air-conditioned for your comfort." Willard Bolchoz, a Horace Heidt Talent Show winner, played around Charleston all his life. Pictured (left to right) are: King Walker, Wes Fern on drums, Willard Bolchoz, Albert Seel and Johnny Goudelock on piano.

Submitted by Rose Bolchoz

Halloween Festivities ◄

The five orange paper lanterns these children were holding at the Shaw Center on Mary Street meant merriment and good times in 1947. From left to right: John Mack, Penzola Williams, Rosetta Hanesworth, Annette McKenzie and Edward Capers. Annette is now Annette McKenzie Anderson, Ph.D., an opera singer; she appeared in a 2008 Piccolo Spoleto Festival event. She is also a speech-language pathologist. Most children in the neighborhood at the time were familiar with the Shaw Center as an educational and fun place for activities. It is now the Boys' and Girls' Club.

Submitted by Delores R. Smith

May Pole Festival ►

Liberty Homes was a small, quiet, friendly neighborhood in North Charleston in 1945, with community grounds like the one pictured here at Liberty Homes School. The May Pole Festival was a colorful display usually held the first day of May; it featured elementary school children dancing in and out of each other to braid the May Pole in a rainbow of ribbons. The boys dressed all in white; the girls' dresses were made of green paper. The colorful celebration was a lovely way to welcome springtime.

Submitted by Jan Perkins

Memminger Girls' Graduation Banquet ▲

The Memminger Class of 1946 celebrated graduation at the Fort Sumter Hotel; most of the 165 graduates were able to attend the event. The mother of one of the graduates, Louise Marks, raised the money for the girls' party. The all-girls' school closed in 1950 but was reopened years later as an elementary school. Dorothy (Ostendorff) Ryan is pictured third from the left at the back. The Fort Sumter Hotel on the Battery has been converted to condominiums.

Submitted by Dorothy Ryan

Supporting the War Effort ◄

Many soldiers were coming through Charleston around 1944, the year before the war ended. Pictured here at the Appel home, 178 St. Philip St., is Fannie Appel (bottom step), Rosalie Goldstein (middle step) and Julie Oxler (top step) with three soldiers from World War II.

Submitted by Fannie Rones

Butterflies Beautiful ▲

Mary Lou Murray (left), Emily Green and Marie Sturke were a sweet trio in the early 1940s. The girls studied dance under Mayme E. Forbes, whose studio was in the old Charleston Hotel. Pictured here at Emily Green's home on Bee Street, the girls practiced their recital performance held at Memminger Auditorium.

Submitted by Mary Lou Coombs

Sacrifices of a Soldier ▲

Joe Wolfe, age 5, lived in Liberty Homes with his mother in 1947. Other dads were home from the war by that time; Joe's father, however, was a career Army man, stationed in Germany. He returned about once a year. Joe's father was an escort officer during the Nuremberg Trials. He spent 28 years in the service, reaching the rank of captain.

Submitted by Ann Wolfe

Edgewater Home ◀

Julius and Marie Louise (Puckhaber) Jahnz owned a country home overlooking the Stono River and Elliott's Cut. Known as Edgewater Point, their six acres on the intracoastal waterway featured gardens, stables and of course, plenty of water access with 1,100 feet of frontage. Pictured left to right are: Mrs. Hulda J. Cappelmann, John D. Cappelmann, Mrs. Marie Louise P. Jahnz, Mrs. Aline Bollman.

Submitted by John Coombs

Dick Ellison and His Debonairs

In 1941 County Hall, 1000 King St., was new; it was the place to go for boxing and the box step. Dick Ellison and His Debonairs, a group of Charleston High School students, was the first dance band to perform there. Front row (left to right): Reginald Nepveux, Costa Palassis, Wardie Alford, Dr. Ernest Horres, Dick Ellison, Dick Riggs. Back row: Johnny Misoyianis, Herchel Hudson, Dr. Abner Levkoff.

Submitted by Johnny Misoyianis

Neither Wind, Nor Rain… ◄

Nor the 1940 hurricane will keep George Walker from visiting his newborn daughter Brenda at the original St. Francis Xavier Infirmary, on the corner of Calhoun Street and Ashley Avenue. Mr. Walker had to borrow a rowboat to make the trip "by sea." The hurricane hit Aug. 11, 1940. Hurricanes were not named at that time, but it was estimated at a Category 2.

Submitted by Brenda Walker Reeves

Downtown Flooded ▶

This photo, taken from an upper-story window, shows Smith and Beaufain streets after the 1940 hurricane. The water is knee-high on the person in the background.

From estate of the late Rev. Msgr. John Fleming McManus, submitted by Caroline Alexander

A Sound Group of Men ◄

The Charleston Federation of Musicians Concert Band, led by George Johnson on the left, was probably in Hampton Park for a concert in the summer of 1947.
Submitted by Alice Weil

Piering Back in Time ◄

It is a trip down memory lane to July, 1940 when E. DuBose Blakeney, III was a 3-year-old and the Folly pier was a bustling place to visit. Next to DuBose are his aunt Sarah Ann Bissell and his mother Frances Bissell Blakeney.
Submitted by E. DuBose Blakeney, III

Fill'er Up ►

Making a stop to fill the tank is nothing unusual, unless the tank you're filling is a Johnson outboard at the Texaco station on the corner of Ashley and Wentworth streets. In October 1947, before storms were named, high tide meant high-test for the boat, not the car, if you wanted to get around. John Rodgers is pictured filling up Bobby Burdell's tank with Texaco Sky Chief.
Submitted by Claudia FitzGerald

Tailored Sailor ▼

Two-year-old David Ott had his very own, authentic sailor suit in 1941; the uniform had belonged to his Uncle Charlie and had been cut down to fit little David. The photo was taken outside the family home at 90 Queen St.

Submitted by David Ott

Bulldog Ball ▲

Richard Brewer (second from the left on the bottom row) was a Knob in 1948, attending The Citadel on a football scholarship. His all-around athleticism led him to play baseball too. Brewer majored in business administration and joined the Air Force after college.

Submitted by Mary Brewer

May Procession ▲

Sacred Heart Church on King Street held a May Procession each year to honor the Virgin Mary. These four cousins participated in 1947. Left to right: Joan Smith, Celestine "Tuney" Couturier, Barbara Smith, Andera Ritter.

Submitted by Celeste Cornell

Shipping Out ▼

Joseph I. Williams, Jr. (left) and his uncle Robert were ready to ship out to the Atlantic Theater in 1942, just after Pearl Harbor. They are pictured here in their Navy uniforms at the family's Chapel Street home.

Submitted by Joe Williams

Catching the Limit ▽

These gentlemen certainly had a good day at the black fish banks in 1946. Red Graves (left), Wendell Zimmerman, James Maher and Jim Jackson enjoyed going fishing off shore.

Submitted by Doris Maher Richards

"Nicaragua Victory" Crashes Into Grace Bridge in 1946 ▲

Brenda Reeves was only 6 years old at the time, but she will never forget returning to the city with her parents when a freighter crashed through the bridge, collapsing the bridge deck and roadway and sending a family of five to their deaths just five cars ahead of them. For months after the accident, the only means into Charleston from Mount Pleasant was by ferry or driving around via Moncks Corner.

Submitted by Brenda Walker Reeves

The Pregnancy Coat ▲

Dorothy "Boots" Chapman said any time she had that coat on, she was pregnant. She is pictured here in 1947 at Colonial Lake with her husband Ray and one of their children, somewhere beneath that coat. Chapman, a cook in the Navy, met his wife while he was stationed in Charleston. The family lived a few blocks away from Colonial Lake, on Queen Street; Mrs. Chapman enjoyed getting her exercise by walking to the park.

Submitted by Judy Chapman

Beginning of a Long Romance ◄

Buck Smith used to "date" Betty Karr by walking her home from the theater, but on this occasion they double-dated with someone who had a car. For that reason they consider this trip to Folly Beach in 1941 their first real date. They married two years later and enjoyed 63 years together.

Submitted by Mary Brewer

Bishop England Buddies ▲

Margaret Shahid, Virginia Comar, Mary Ann Runey and Helen Dodds were school friends who spent some happy times at Folly Beach in the mid-1940s. The girls are pictured under the "Folly Pier Dancing" sign. The sign to the right instructs drivers to "drive slow—10 mph—underneath the pier."

Submitted by Anne Comar Willis

Row, Row, Row the Boat ▲

James Maher, a lighthouse inspector, brought home a lifeboat that the Coast Guard had found at sea. Betty (Terry) Thompson and her friend Doris (Maher) Richards lived on Smith Street in 1944. They spent many days and evenings on Colonial Lake, but this photo captured one of the few times Betty actually rowed the boat.

Submitted by Doris Maher Richards

1950s

A Head (and an Arm) For Business

When J.C. Long asked Henry J. Brown, Jr. if his son would like his old wagon, which had been used for picking up the family cleaning, Brown gladly accepted. After cutting it down so young H.J. Brown, III could see over the top, it was renamed the "Humphrey Wagon," based on a Joe Palooka character. H. J. Brown, pictured here at age 15 in 1952, delivered newspapers for many years to the northern part of the city.

Submitted by Henry Brown, III

Coast-to-Coast Road Trip ◄

Melvin Bessinger needed a vacation. In 1954 he was working 18 hours a day at his restaurant, "Eat at Joe's," in Holly Hill. Thanks to his best friend, Paul Moore, and his younger brother, Thomas Bessinger, Melvin was able to take five weeks off for a road trip in his 1951 pink Cadillac Seville. Going along for the ride were his nephew Ronnie Boals (left), Bessinger's mother and his aunt. They drove to California first and then to New York City. Bessinger's son Melvin David Bessinger now runs the two Melvin's Legendary BBQ restaurants in Mount Pleasant and James Island.

Submitted by Melvin David Bessinger

The Birthday Hat Ladies ►

It was a rousing 17th birthday party for Mary Catherine Farabow at her family's home in Riverland Terrace in 1956. No complaints were filed by neighbors, however. The girls have been friends since first grade and theirs was the first graduating class of James Island High School in 1957. Left to right: AnnJi (Hund) Salley, Carolyn (Shokes) Sime, Louise Farabow (hatless mother of the birthday girl), Rosalyn (Crawford) Simmons, Nancy (Wilkins) Blakeney, Mary Catherine Farabow and Kitty (Jones) Reid.

Submitted by Nancy Blakeney

Photo Opportunity ▲

If a picture says a thousand words, then all one thousand words of this photograph would be "love," in as many different ways as the emotion can be expressed. William Charles Kilpatrick and his wife Cecil R. Kilpatrick took the opportunity to give each other a hug in 1955 at the Isle of Palms. The sweethearts were doing a little fishing close to Breach Inlet.

Submitted by Carol Biering

Oyster Roast, Jaycees-Style ▲

When these friends got together, they got things done for the community, and had fun doing it. Pictured here in 1954 are West Ashley Junior Chamber of Commerce members and their wives (left to right): Larry Bryant, Hugh Turner, Pug Turner, Joanne Easterby, Hugh Easterby, Pat Shiver, Blanche Brown, Barbara Philips, Betty Anne Bryant.

Submitted by Betty Anne Bryant

Waiting for the Dance Music To Start ▲

Arnold Bennett, age 19, waited on a bench at the old Folly Pier in the summer of 1958. It wasn't quite time for the bands to strike up yet, so he made himself at home. The bench advertised, "Jim" and someone whose name began with "D" apparently offering a burger and beer combo for 25 cents. If you want golden (French?) fries you'd have to cough up another 15 cents. Bennett's family owned a home at Folly in the '40s and '50s, but continued to frequent the family beach, for weeks at a time or just for the day, long after their home was sold.

Submitted by Irene Bennett

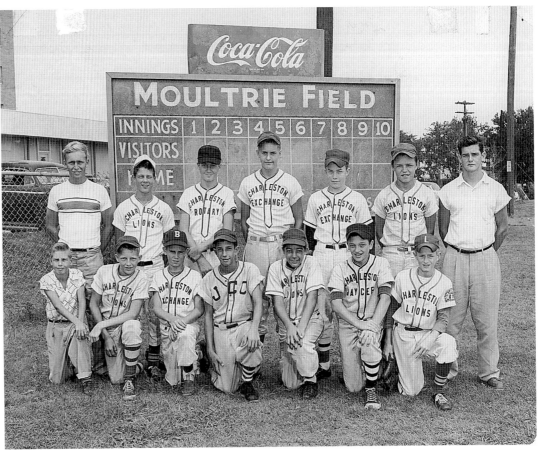

Pony League All-Stars ▲

Representing teams such as the Lions, Rotary, Exchange, Jaycees and the JCC, these 13- and 14-year-old boys were peninsula all-stars in 1953. Pictured on Moultrie playground are (first row, left to right): Rudy Howell, Richard Goehring, Fred McMahon, Haskel Toporek, Ronnie Barrineau, Eddie Bendt, Nolan Schwerin. Second row: Walter Prause (coach), Crow Moseley, Ed Good, Allan Millar, Sonny Phillips, Bernard Ackerman, Johnny Easterby (coach). Not present for the photo were: Heyward Harvey, Lloyd Walters, Bobby O'Brien, Bobby Cathcart.

Submitted by Jerry McMahon

Mouth-Watering Watermelon ▲

The great thing about watermelon at the beach is that if the juice runs down your arm, it is easily rinsed off with an afternoon swim. It was a Petit family tradition to rent a house at Folly every year. Pictured here enjoying large slices in 1953 (from left to right) are: Linda, Ann, Susan, Marjorie and Buddy Petit (in front).

Submitted by Linda Lassiter

Catch of the Day ▲

Pop Keller loved to fish Lake Moultrie and would often drive to his grandchildren's home in Morningside subdivision with the "catch of the day." Pictured with their grandfather in 1953 are Kenney (left), Susie and Terry Keller.

Submitted by Susie Childress

Hirsch Wholesale ▲

Back in the 1950s Hirsch Wholesale, 157 East Bay St., sold candy and notions such as thread and socks, to corner groceries and country stores. Pictured outside the company (top row from left to right) are: Abe Klein, Danny Hirsch, Mrs. Klein, Sylvia Hirsch, Max Hirsch. Bottom row: David Lancer, Murray Lancer, Betty Lancer.

Submitted by Betty Hirsch Lancer

Fireman's Prayer ▼

James Hogan Lloyd, Jr. is pictured kneeling beside his bed at Central Station, corner of Meeting and Wentworth streets, in the early 1950s. Firemen worked 24 hours on and 24 hours off; a fireman had to be ready to jump into his boots, quite literally, when the alarm sounded.

Submitted by Doris Lloyd

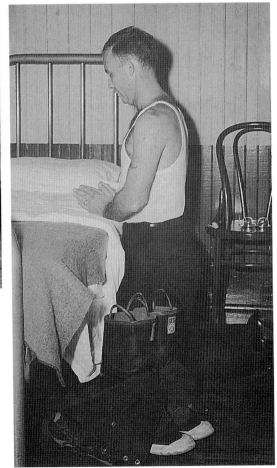

Drive-In Banking West of the Ashley ▲

Cecil B. Kearse, cashier of the Citizens and Southern National Bank's West Ashley Branch, presented Mrs. Lewis M. Denaux with a potted camellia for being the first customer in the bank's new drive-in office in Avondale in 1956. Kearse worked with C & S from 1947–1981, retiring as vice-president. Ruth DeStefano is the teller in the window.

Submitted by Cecil Kearse

Everything's Relative ▶

Bernadette (Richards) Knisley, Irene (Richards) Bennett and their niece Jill (Richards) Johnson stand in front of the Richards' home on Alexander Street in 1951. Little Jill lived on Society Street and was visiting her aunts. She is holding an alphabet book entitled, "From A To Z."

Submitted by Bernadette Knisley

Girl Talk ▲

The girls got together at the home of Mr. and Mrs. Paul Gigis on Rutledge Avenue to help GeeGee (Pavlis) Manutes borrow just the right dress. GeeGee was in the Queen's Court for the Miss St. Andrews Beauty Contest for St. Andrews High School in the mid-1950s. Pictured (left to right): Kathrine (Gigis) Theos, Pauline (Pavlis) Phillips, Barbara (Gigis) Latto, Mary Susan (Jackson) Davenport, GeeGee (Pavlis) Manutes, Anna (Phillips) Melissas.

Submitted by GeeGee Manutes

(New) Courtenay School Graduates ▲

The seventh-grade class of the "new" Courtenay school, located at the site of the "old" Courtenay school on Meeting and Mary streets, received their diplomas in 1958. Those who could be identified include: Barbara Griffin, Joe Knight, James Parker, Raymond Benton, Rose Dehay, Charles Jaegar, Faye Phillips, Carol Hilton, Edward White, Marion Wright, Patsy D'Angelo, Bobby Singletary, James Peagler and Clarence Woodard.

Submitted by Joseph Knight, Jr.

Harley's Meat Market ▶

Carl Harley, pictured here at his store at 171 Spring St., spent 37 years at that location. He began his career in the meat business at a Radcliffe Street market when he was just 13 years old. Harley's Meat Market offered a delivery service; many of his customers requested that the deliverymen come into their homes while they were away and put their orders in the refrigerator.

Submitted by Sandra Jones

Roper Nursing Student Junior Class Officers ▲

Gloria Cook, Joyce Ray, Anne (Welling) Knox and Carolyn (Caveny) Matthews (left to right) were in their second year of nursing in 1952, as indicated by a single stripe on the cap. The girls lived in Riverside Nurses Home, which was a hospital at one time. Anne Knox was born there in 1933. Students routinely worked the 3 p.m. to 7 a.m. shift at old Roper Hospital, a shift manned only by registered nurse supervisors and interns.

Submitted by Anne Knox

The First "R" ▲

Of the three "Rs," "reading" comes first because it is the foundation of all learning. Mrs. Bartley Bull, well-loved teacher at Craft School on Legare and Queen streets, made sure reading was fun as well. Pictured here in a first grade reading group, 1950, from left to right, are: Robert Newton, Nelson Merrill, Laura Swan, Whit Smith, David Humphreys, Sammy Cothran, Mrs. Bull, Albert Bonnoit. Craft School has been converted to condominiums.

Submitted by Mrs. David Humphreys

Come To A Card Party ◄

Annabelle Goehring (left) and Beverly Craven were volunteers raising money for the Florence Crittenton Home in the early 1950s. The event held at the Fort Sumter Hotel, included games of all sorts, a fashion show, hors d'oeuvres and drinks. Florence Crittenton has been a place for single pregnant women on St. Margaret Street since 1897.

Submitted by Annabelle R. Jenkins

Surveying Gracie's Damage ▲

Arnold and Irene (Richards) Bennett married the year
Hurricane Gracie visited Charleston in September
1959. They lived at 4 Franklin St., just north of Broad
Street. After the hurricane hit in September, the
Bennetts and some friends took a trip to the old "Yacht
Basin," the marina located across the street from
Roper Hospital on Calhoun.

Submitted by Irene Bennett

Island-Hopping ▲

Leona Marie Fender (left) and her sister Nellie Bly
Morris visited Isle of Palms in 1954. The women often
visited IOP and Sullivan's Island because according to
family records their Irish ancestors, the O'Sullivans,
figured quite prominently in island history.

Submitted by Lois Krakeel

Scouting Out Cookie Sales ▲

Gail (Young) Carter, on the left, and her sister Judy
took advantage of their father's place of employment
on the Charleston Naval Base when it was cookie-
selling season. Judy said the best time to sell cookies
was on Friday paydays; employees would cash their
checks and then walk outside where the girls were
ready for customers. Gail was almost 13 in 1955 and
Judy was 11. Cookies sold for 50 cents a box.

Submitted by Judy Young Hall

American Legion Drum & Bugle Corps ▲

Donald R. Houghtaling (left front, with glasses) took part in the Azalea Day Parade on King Street in 1955. He belonged to the American Legion, which was on Society Street. Some of the businesses on King at that time were Maxwell Brothers Furniture, Rustin's and Eleanor's.

Submitted by Lorraine Houghtaling

Let's Eat! ▲

Everyone brought a dish for family picnics at Uncle Johnny Roessler's house in the late 1950s. He is pictured at the far left. His property included shady pecan trees, a creek with a dock for fishing, and a windmill. The Houghtalings, Roesslers, Coles and Thompsons enjoyed their summer get-togethers there.

Submitted by Lorraine Houghtaling

Taking the Plunge ◄

Morris Finkelstein loved sports—all sports. He coached basketball, swimming and track at Charleston High School. Shown here in the mid-1950s, Coach Finkelstein helped Henry Viohl with his dive at the municipal pool that used to be off George Street. David Stuhr is behind Viohl, watching his technique.

Submitted by Sarah Finkelstein

Dogpatch, USA ▲

Li'l Abner and Daisy Mae Scragg brought Dogpatch to Charleston at the Azalea Festival in 1952. Pictured here on the Battery, holding hands and a bag containing their First Place prize, are Angela Schiffiano and her Li'l Abner.

Submitted by James Cooper

"Enter To Learn, Leave to Serve" ▼

Coach Morris Finkelstein took the words inscribed over the old Charleston High School's entrance to heart, and he taught those values to the athletes he coached. Pictured here are Coach Finkelstein and members of the 1958 Charleston Bantam Track Team. First row (left to right) is: Alfred Pinckney, Skipper Ogletree, Harry Bishop, Henry Viohl. Second row: John Hope, Capers Poulnot, Robert Burns. The school's facade and inscription remain today, encouraging all those who enter MUSC's College of Health Professions.

Submitted by Sarah Finkelstein

Polio in the 1950s ◂

When 2-year-old Susie Keller came down with the viral infection known as polio in 1954, the vaccine was only given to 4th-graders because there wasn't enough to go around. She spent 21 days in isolation at Roper Hospital. She recovered from polio eventually; after years of physical therapy and wearing a brace on her left leg, and later, a built-up shoe, the bones in her right leg stopped growing and the left leg caught up. She is fine today. Susie is pictured in her grandfather's arms, Pop Keller, with her mother Annette Keller at her side.

Submitted by Susie Childress

The Petits at Rutledge ▴

Lester Petit owned a heating and air business at 511 Rutledge Ave. in 1956. The family lived above the business. Pictured on the left is Ann Petit; next to Mr. Petit is his wife Juanita, with Linda Petit beside her. Seated are Susan, Bobbie and Buddy.

Submitted by Linda Lassiter

It Gets Me To the Office and Back ▸

Frederica Green can barely see over the door from her father's Austin-Healey convertible in 1956. She was 3 years old, and her family lived at 75 South Battery at the time. Her father, L. Louis Green, III, designed and built the house using architectural salvage including floors from the Charleston Orphanage and the front door fanlight from a house on Chalmers Street. Green was president of the Charleston Shipyard.

Submitted by Frederica Mathewes-Green

Pizza—What's That?

Hard to believe, but in the mid-1950s many people had never heard of pizza. So when Leonard LaBrasca opened LaBrasca's Pizzeria on King Street, he asked these three adorable Pizza Queens to educate folks. Betty Ann LaBrasca (left) and Pansy LaBrasca (behind her) helped Sheryle Bolton, Ramona LaBrasca and Donna LaBrasca (right) pass out samples. LaBrasca's Pizzeria expanded to several locations in Charleston and one in Columbia, S.C.; the King Street restaurant was next door to The Spaghetti House, owned by Essie and George LaBrasca, Sr.

Submitted by Ramona LaBrasca

That's Amore

"When the moon hits your eye like a big-a pizza pie…" The lyrics to Dean Martin's song are apropos for this couple: George LaBrasca, Jr., (left) is the son of Essie and George LaBrasca, Sr., who owned The Spaghetti House on King Street. George, Jr. made a career in the family business, doing bookkeeping for the restaurants and opening the LaBrasca's Pizzeria location in Columbia. He married Pansy in 1950. The couple is pictured on Folly Beach.

Submitted by Ramona LaBrasca

Come, Mr. Tally Man ◄

Adele Jennings Baker displayed the bananas grown in the sheltered walled garden of her home at 10 Meeting St. Mrs. Baker was married to Dr. Archibald E. Baker, founder of Baker Sanatorium on Colonial Lake at Ashley Avenue and Beaufain Street. "Mama Baker" was quite the gardener; she had a glass-walled room she called the "conservatory" where she grew orchids and other plants. In this photo, taken around 1950, Mrs. Baker would have been about 85 years old.

Submitted by Mary Baker Pringle

New Building for Courtenay School Children ▲

When Stan Mizell (back row, third from left) went to first grade in 1956, Courtenay was a brand new school. The new school was built on the same site as the original school, dating back to 1888. Recollections are that the adults from left to right are: Ms. Cuney, Ms. Cannon, Principal Gibbes and Room Mother Mrs. Manos.

Submitted by Stan Mizell

Safety Beneficial Program ▼

As part of an awareness event in May 1955, the Navy Yard provided entertainment and lunch to highlight the importance of safety. The singing trio of Evelyn Cutrell (left), Jean Lee and Jan Esco Mizell, a secretary at the shipyard, were part of the afternoon festivities.

Submitted by Jan Perkins

Photo With the Fire Chief ▲

When the St. Andrews Fire Chief came through Riverland Terrace in February 1951, 6-year-old Chet Nowak got his picture taken with him. The other child is unidentified.

Submitted by Chet Nowak

Ott Brothers ◄

Edward Ott is in the arms of his big brother David in 1951 at the family's home, 29 Saratoga Road. The boys' father, Samuel D. Ott, was a Charleston city policeman. The family lived there until 1954, when the city began requiring police officers to live within the city limits. The family moved to Moultrie Street.

Submitted by David Ott

Seaside Siblings ◄

Angus Baker, Jr. and his sister Mary enjoyed their childhood summers on Sullivan's Island, roaming the beach, collecting shells, and developing a love for the ocean and the creatures that live in it. The Baker family summerhouse at 2508 I'on Ave., was affectionately named "Sleepy Hollow" because it was such a relaxing place to be—naps were inevitable.

Submitted by Mary Baker Pringle

Palmetto Outboard Club ▲

The love of power boat racing was the viscous agent that held these men together in the 1950s. Members raced against each other in various classes according to engine horsepower: from 5 HP up to 30 HP. Sunday afternoons in the summer were spent at various liquid locations statewide. Pictured are Robert Mizzel, Danny Winter, Joe Deytens, Buddy Puckhaber, Walter Prause, Jack Smoak, Stumpy Curry, Lawrence Collins, Louis Westin, John Glover, Tux Glover, John Gardner, Jennings Lucas, Rudy Rustin, Charlie Fabian, A.W. Smoak, Commodore Hogg, Dan Pickett.

Submitted by George Puckhaber

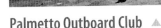

There's a New Sheriff In Town ▶

Van Noy Thornhill portrayed Wild Bill Hickok at the Carolina Yacht Club's Fancy Dress Ball in February, 1951. Wild Bill kept the peace that evening, and reportedly made sure he was not seated with his back facing an open door.

Submitted by Jane Thornhill

Azalea Queen and Entourage ▲

The Azalea Festival parade grew tremendously over the years, but in this photo it was still just a small event beginning at East Bay Playground and ending on the High Battery. The Queen, Sister (Dotterer) Rutledge (left) is attended by her court: Julie (Pritchard) Hyde, Tommy, Jackie and David Maybank (representing dignitaries such as Senator Maybank and Governor Byrnes), and marshals Sam Applegate and William Wilson, decked out in their Boy Scout uniforms for the occasion.

Submitted by Leslie D. (Sister) Rutledge

Four Generations ▲

Edward Preston Mazyck (left) owned a cotton farm off Ashley Phosphate in the 1950s. He gave the city the rights to build a road on his land and, in return, the city named a road after him. Next to Edward is LeRoy Alexander Mazyck, LeRoy, Jr., and LeRoy, III.

Submitted by Daisy Adeline McMillan Mazyck

Immaculate Conception School 4th Grade Class ▼

It's just the boys, pictured here in 1954. The girls were photographed separately. The Catholic school on Coming Street was taught by all black nuns. It is now a senior citizen building. Those who could be identified on the first row (left to right) are: Arthur Lewis, Frances Wright, William Amos, Julius Amaker, Herman Lum, Rodney Briggs. Second row: Robert Drayton, Charles Stent, Berlin Simmons, Frank Godfrey, Eugene Perry, Marcellus Singleton, Henry Gilbert. Third row: Eugene Collier, Harry Holmes, Frank Hamilton, Richard Gethers, James Walker, Herman Montague, O'Neil Gant.

Submitted by Maxine Poindexter

Ground-Breaking Doctors ▲

Dr. Turner McCottry and Dr. Catherine McCottry began practicing at McClennan Banks Hospital on Cannon Street. In the 1950s black physicians were denied the right to admit and care for patients in white hospitals. The McCottrys began their medical careers at the Cannon Street Hospital; they helped to integrate hospitals during their practice even after McClennan Banks Memorial Hospital opened on Courtenay Drive in 1959. This 31-bed facility operated until 1976; the site is now the new Ashley Towers.

Submitted by Cynthia McCottry Smith

Lunch Time on The Bedouin ▲

Jane Thornhill (left), Mary Mahoney, Bee Hutson, and an unidentified woman are ready for lunch in 1951 aboard The Bedouin.

Submitted by Jane Thornhill

The Keg on King ▲

"Ma" Herman (left) and her husband Willie owned and operated the little bar at 318 King St. in the 1950s. Manning the tap in the photo is Gilbert F. Ryan, Naval Supply Center worker by day, and bartender occasionally at night and on Saturdays. The reindeer and dollar bills in the background were part of a Christmas charity.

Submitted by Mike Young

Wedding Bells for Carrolls ▲

Florine Brown met Arthur Carroll at Burke Industrial High School. He graduated in 1946; she graduated three years later, with the first class to finish Burke in the 12th grade. Until 1949 students graduated after 11 years of education. Carroll went into the army, but they kept in touch; Florine and Arthur were married in 1950.

Submitted by Deborah Shaif

Growing up on Maverick ▶

Mike Young (left) and his brother George were pals with the Karesh brothers, Charles and Steve, when the families lived on Maverick Street. As is evident by their footwear, the Karesh boys' father made his living in shoes. Mike and George's father did not. The boys enjoyed playing at Hampton Park playground, which is now known as McMahon playground.

Submitted by Mike Young

The Bedouin

Charleston Oil Company owned a houseboat in the 1950s and every autumn several men took her out for a cruise, at a cost of $10 per person. This particular outing took them to Otto Island for marsh hen hunting. Pictured left to right: Ab Middleton, Henry Smythe, Elliot Hutson, Buddy Smith, Laurance Stoney, Palmer Gaillard, John McCrady.

Submitted by Jane Thornhill

Sippin' Soda ▲

The girls at Murray Vocational High School on Chisholm Street had a break from school so they walked across the street to Sgt. Jasper Apartments for sodas in 1953. The school educated men and women in such skills as typing, auto mechanics and drafting. Pictured at left: Jean Moore with Shirley Stehmeier behind her. Pictured at right: Joyce Massalon with Meg Gothe behind her. The girls and a dozen other close friends still stay in touch, getting together once a month to travel or just to have fun.

Submitted by Shirley Stehmeier Winter

Grandmother's Sweet Shop ◄

Harry Wright (left) with his cousin James Jenkins and sister Meta Wright (right) stood in front of their grandmother's Sweet Shop, 221 Coming St. in 1955. The children's grandmother sold cookies, and also link bologna and fresh cut meats at the business. Before Brooks Motor Inn was built, she also ran a boarding house at this location.

Submitted by Meta Waldon

Womanless Wedding ▲

In the early 1950s the Womanless Wedding was a good-natured, funny and entertaining way to raise money for charities. It was wholesome entertainment for the whole family. Pictured here as one of the "bridesmaids" is Frank McMahon, Sr. with his sons Sidney (left) and Pat (right). McMahon is holding Rial "Buddy" Fitch, Jr.

Submitted by Betty Stelljes

Senior Beach Party ▲

The 1954 graduating class of Murray Vocational School celebrated their accomplishment over a weekend at Folly Beach—boys in one house, girls in another. Roughly 50 students graduated that year; the weekend included swimming and a cookout. Joyce Massalon is pictured on the left, next to Shirley Stehmeier.

Submitted by Shirley Stehmeier Winter

"P" is for "Post" ◄

Betty Stelljes went to work for the newspaper when the business was located at 134 Meeting St. In 1952, when the company moved to 134 Columbus St., the newspaper's two mastheads were displayed on the side of the building. The "P" would be used for *The Evening Post*, the paper's afternoon newspaper. She is pictured sitting on the counter in the Classified Department.

Submitted by Betty Stelljes

Lunch Is Served ▲

Duncan Hayes Weeks, Sr. was the head of The Citadel Mess Hall in 1957. He was responsible for all school-related parties and also catered for Gen. Mark Clark. He is pictured with the staff at a luncheon held at The Citadel Beach House on Isle of Palms.

Submitted by Beth Weeks Galt

Pint-Sized Residence and Ride ▲

A child-sized home deserves a child-sized car. The doll house pictured in the Thornhills' yard, 24 Legare St., came from one of the children's grandmother's house in Summerville. The Thornhill boys enjoyed camping out and hosting oyster roasts there.

Submitted by Jane Thornhill

Riverland Terrace Windmill ▶

John Roessler built the windmill pictured on the back of his property at 2028 Wappoo Hall Road near Wappoo Creek. His niece isn't sure why he built it; she remembers it as a dirty place that smelled of oil and machinery. Later, the windmill was moved from his home to Plymouth Park. Grace Cole is pictured in the bottom window; Madeline Houghtaling (left) and Ida Cole peer out of the top window.

Submitted by Lorraine Houghtaling

Community-Oriented Mary McNeal ▲

Mary McNeal, pictured at the back on the left, owned a florist shop on Spring Street. She is remembered for her big green station wagon with four bench seats—the one that took neighborhood children on outings of all sorts, including the Lucky 2 Ranch on Channel 2 in the summer of 1955. Meta Wright is on the first row, third from the right. Her brother Harry is next to her. Tony Glenn, the cowboy host of the show, is kneeling on the far right.

Submitted by Meta Waldon

Rivers High Senior Board ▲

The newly elected Senior Board of Rivers High celebrated election returns at Faulkner Drug Store on King Street in 1959. Pictured (left to right) are: Treasurer Tommy Walters, Secretary Helen Rhea, Vice-President Robert Goldstein and President Larry Bailey.

Submitted by Tommy Walters

Momeier Paint Store ▲

Walter W. Momeier, Sr. owned the store at 412 Meeting St. in 1959, it was sold a few years after this photograph was taken. The store specialized in general paints and building supplies.

Submitted by Greta Waters

Tearful Good-Bye ◄

When Tommy Chears said good-bye to his wife Lois (Johnston) Chears in December 1959, he knew he would not see her for quite a while. Chears was shipping out to Okinawa for 19 months; the couple had been married about six months at that time. Chears spent more than three years in the Army; they are pictured here at the old airport in North Charleston.

Submitted by Lois Johnston Chears

There's Nothing Like Family ◄

Of the 35 first cousins who grew up together in Charleston, these four were inseparable. Pictured at the Battery in the late 1950s are (left to right): Mike Peeples, Ray Heissenbuttle, Ralph Peeples, Jr. and Roy Heissenbuttle. The Heissenbuttles lived downtown on Logan Street but the rest of the family grew up within one square mile of each other, in Avondale, Byrnes Downs and Ashley Forest. Birthdays and family celebrations, needless to say, were rarely low-key events.

Submitted by Martha Attisano

Bell's Esso at Ten Mile Hill ◄

At the corner of Rivers and Remount, Bell's Esso serviced most of the population in that busy area beginning in the early 1950s. Full service with a smile also included whisk-brooming customers' cars. Pictured is the 22-year-old owner, J.E. Bell, Sr. pumping 21-cents-per-gallon gasoline into his 1951 Cadillac. After Hurricane Gracie in 1959, Bell's Esso was the only operating service station within miles that pumped gas with a generator. Bell's Esso is now Gerald's Tires.

Submitted by J.E. Bell, Jr.

Fifty Years and Counting ◄

Caroline Maria Walker married George B. Alexander March 20, 1958. The wedding ceremony took place at Sacred Heart Church with a reception following at Caroline's grandmother's home. The couple took a weekend honeymoon in Jacksonville and went to work immediately afterward but 50 years later, they made up for it by taking a belated honeymoon trip to Niagara Falls.

Submitted by George B. Alexander

The Turner Family ▲

Mary Jane Heyward Turner, pictured in the center with her family around her at 39 Mary St., finished Avery Normal Institute on Bull Street and taught school on the islands. Her husband, who was a fireman on the railroad, died some years earlier. Back row (left to right): Mamie E. Turner, Daniel A. Turner, Lucille Turner McCottry, Andy McDonald McCottry. Front row: Robert L. Turner, Christopher Turner (Mikie).

Submitted by Cynthia McCottry Smith

Stellar Stellings ▼

These three brothers have always been close; Jim (left), Gerard and Robert are 7, 9 and 5 in 1958 and the best of pals, then and now. Each set records for swimming in their youth: one for breast stroke and butterfly, another for endurance swimming and the third for diving. But on this day the boys enjoyed just hanging out in their dungarees and riding bikes. They all attended Watt School on Broad Street, and then Gaud School at a time when dungarees were not permitted in school.

Submitted by Anne Allison

Turkey Day Relay Races ▲

Every year Coach Morris Finkelstein took his track and basketball teams to the Knights of Columbus Turkey Day Relay Races at the Battery. Coach Finkelstein's basketball team ran just like the track team; he stressed fundamentals and conditioning in all the sports he coached. The team is shown with their winnings for the day. Those who could be identified on the track team include, front row, left to right: Henry Siegling, Jimmy Black, Frank Robson, Billy Burns, Alfred Pinckney, Larry Walker. Those who could be identified on the basketball team, back row, include: Billy Silcox, John Doyle, Jimmy Taylor, John Townsend, Michael Tenratis, Clarence Ray, Owen Ravenel, Bill Yarbrough, Dave Sykes, Teddy Englemann, Billy Key.

Submitted by Billy Silcox

Parent Participation Trophy ◄

Mrs. Selma D. Caldwell's third grade class at A. B. Rhett Elementary School was proud to win the PTA contest in 1952 for parent participation. Displaying their award is Evelyn (Whaley) Miller. The building still stands on President Street, across the street from the current Burke High School. Back row (left to right): Vivian Grant, Ann Ladson, Johnie Mae Ash. Front row: Emma Ashby, Blondell Lee, Walter Burke, Wilhelmina Michel, Carolyn Pembroke, Kenneth Goff, Penelope Wright, Henrietta Brown.

Submitted by Evelyn Miller

1953 First Graders ▶

All the first-grade classes of James Simons Elementary School, corner of King and Moultrie streets, are pictured here in 1953. Maria Kirlis' family had just emigrated from Greece two years earlier; Maria was just learning to speak English when she began school but she never missed a day and she was never tardy. Her father owned Rainbow Restaurant at the main gate of the naval base. He cooked nothing but Greek food and the sailors kept the place packed.

Submitted by Maria Kirlis Bornhorst

James Island 4th-Grade Roll Call ▽

Betty McMichael (standing in the back, next to the open windows) was in her third year of teaching in 1959. She taught a total of 38 years on James Island. Her classroom shows their studies of birds and their habitats, a terrarium, as well as assignments for an upcoming Field Day, including a tug of war and 50-yard dash. Students who could be identified include: Randy Jenkins, Mary Mood, Danny Carson, Gene Cox, Norman Doudiet. Vernon K. Williams was the principal.

Submitted by Betty McMichael

Sittin' Pretty ▲

Dee Meador wasn't able to climb a tree at 1 year of age, but he could sit and hold on for dear life. Little Dee was placed in the tree in front of his grandparents' home in Garco Village for picture-taking in 1958. Grandparents Harry and Anna Harbeson lived at 106 Gaffney St. in North Charleston; the neighborhood at that time was full of hard-working people who looked out for one another. Everyone had front porches where friends and family gathered in the afternoon for conversation. Dee's grandfather was a sheet metal worker at Garco.

Submitted by Janell Meador

East Bay Elementary's First Faculty ◄

Today the school is Sanders-Clyde, but in 1955 it was East Bay Elementary, and it was brand new. The faculty (first row, left to right) are: Ophelia Frierson Wright, Louise Cole, Christina Greenwood Jakes, Wilmot J. Fraser, principal, Ruby MacBeth, Ida Tobias Jackson, Lucia Brown, Cecile Bowman. Second row: Alma Jones, Thelma Washington, Edena Green Deas, Louise Middleton Palmer, Thomisena Boone Mouzon, Juliette Mack Graham, Emma J. Alston. Third row: Margaret Smith, Margaret Marshall Wainwright, Euphrasia Lewis, Dorothy Wilson Ashe, Raymond Rhett, Marie Robinson, Evelyn Nelson Young, Verbatine Lawrence Davis. Fourth row: Mary Wright, secretary, Septima Poinsette Clark, James Tolbert, Cynthia McCottry Smith, JoeEthel Middleton Moore.

Submitted by Cynthia McCottry Smith

Leon's Men's Wear ►

Leon Rabin (left) opened his first store in 1939 at 490 King St. but had it not been for a young lady named Ann Mazo, whom he met while traveling in Charleston, the store may have been established in the Northeast. Ann later became his wife. Pictured here about 1951 in front of stacks of men's dress shirts, Mr. Rabin offered premium men's clothing and was a driving force in Charleston's retail industry for almost 60 years.

Submitted by Eileen Sorota

Boxing Boys ◄

In 1955 a group of boys enjoyed recreational boxing at the Jewish Community Center on St. Philip Street. Donald "Rocky" Morillo was 11 years old at the time. He and Ronnie Gibbs were the only two Protestants on the team; Ronnie grew up to be a Golden Glove Champion. In those days, equipment included gloves and a mouth piece; occasionally, for bouts, the boys would receive head gear. Those who could be identified include, bottom row, left to right: Stanley L. Baker, Marty Schwartz, Stephen Brickman, Donald Morillo, Jimmy Manos, Alan Kline, David Levine. Second row: Murray Lancer, Alan Coleman, Nicky Lempesis, Larry Kline, Ira Solomon, Barry Krell, Steven Schwartz, Ronnie Gibbes. Third row: Billy Solomon, Harold Glassberg, Jerry Wearb. Back row: Danny Hirsch, Woody Woodcock, George Lempesis, boxing referee, Danny Berlinsky, coach, Irvin Levkoff, Mike Toporek, Robert J. Wearb, Chris Manos, coach.

Submitted by Donald O. Morillo, Sr.

Pier Pressure ◄

There was no pressure to have a good time in 1950s; just grab a few blankets and head out to Folly Pier. Lillian Wright and Larry Bryant were in their early 20s at the time.

Submitted by Betty Anne Bryant

Cecile Rubin Chapter of Young Judea ▲

The chapter held a final banquet and dance May 17, 1952 at the Jewish Community Center on St. Philip Street. Young Judea was a civic and social group that was part of Hadassah, a Jewish women's organization that is more than 75 years old. Pictured first row (left to right): Evelyn (Sokol) Needle, Sonia (Sokol) Greenberg, Sandra Lee (Kahn) Rosenblum, Evelyn (Lipman) Sarasohn, Irene (Goldman) Taradash. Back row (left to right): Myra (Krawcheck) Read, Elaine (Cohen) Saul, Ruth (Goldstein) Antrim, Rosemary "Binky" (Read) Cohen, Joan (Goldberg) Sarnoff, Lillian Wearb (advisor), Carol (Wearb) Tuck, Elizabeth Ann (Kominers) Soffe, Sandra (Garfinkle) Shapiro, Fredlyn (Kurtz) Schloss, Sharon (Mendelsohn) Toporek.

Submitted by Rosemary R. Cohen

Friends and Family at Folly ▷

The Couturiers rented a house at the beach every year and their daughters, Celestine (left)—or "Tuney," as she is known—and her sister JoAnna (next to her) were allowed to bring a friend. JoAnna took Eileen Calder in 1952; behind Eileen is Tuney's friend Agatha "Sister" Finnigan. The girls' mother, Gertrude Courturier is on the right.

Submitted by Celeste Cornell

Probies at the Main Nurses Home ◁

These "uncapped" girls were in their first of three years at MUSC and Roper Hospital's School of Nursing. After the probie year, an upperclassman would confer caps in an elaborate capping ceremony. They lived at the Main Nurses Home, 316 Calhoun St., while pursuing their education. The building still stands in the middle of MUSC. From left to right: Anne (Welling) Knox, Carolyn (Caveny) Matthews, Nancy (Oates) Baker.

Submitted by Anne Knox

Male Bonding ▼

This was her "crowd" during her teen years, according to Rosemary (Read) Cohen. The friends lived downtown but spent many weekends at Sullivan's Island. Pictured here in 1953 are (top row, left to right): Herbert Rephan, Sidney Davis, Charlie Goldberg, Barry Clarke, Jacques Kierbel, Skippy White. In the center (left to right): Warren Kohn, Barry Bukatman, Alan Glassberg. Bottom row (left to right): Alan Wilensky, Jackie Karesh, Maurice Krawcheck.

Submitted by Rosemary R. Cohen

Aboard the USS McClellan ▲

The destroyer, based at the Charleston Naval Base in June 1953, was preparing for the Navy Reserve summer tour to the Panama Canal for war games. The officer's name is unknown. Pictured left to right, dressed in white, are: J.J. Bishop, R. Willard Seyle, Joseph A. Moluf, Skippy Bolton, Kenny Spence.

Submitted by Lisa Kynoski

Crowning Miss Charleston, 1950 ▲

Jean Anders was crowned Miss Charleston by Mayor William M. Morrison at the County Hall in 1950. Her duties included functioning as "the city's official hostess," but when she married shortly after inauguration, the runner-up, Roberta Carter (No. 13, on the left, next to Anders) took her spot. When the runner-up got married, the crown fell to Peggy (Thompson) Droze, on the right of Anders, two months into the term. Other women of the court were: Alberta Mazyck, Shirley Robinson, Mildred Mack, Joanne Skipper, Betty Momeier, Ann Tovey, Earline Niles, Rachel Newton, Bobbie Jean Gaston, Joye Jenkins, Jean Sweat. Citadel cadet escorts pictured were: Charles Sanders, Elmer Benschotes, Tommy Christiansen, Bobby Zobel, George Dent, Elvin Kennedy, Theo Thompson, Dick Schweers, Herbert Wilcox, Henry Shaffer, Al Tiedemann, Al Stallings, Fritz Cotton, Dick Earle, Bobby Burdell.

Submitted by Peggy Droze

LaBrascas at the Beach ◄

Pansy LaBrasca (left) and her daughter Ramona and their family spent many fun-filled hours at Folly Beach in the late 1950s. Ramona was 5 years old in the photo; the family enjoyed Folly so much that they later bought a house there.

Submitted by Ramona LaBrasca

The Union Club ◄

Members of local #499 were operating engineers in Charleston. These heavy equipment and crane operators worked around town, many at West Virginia Pulp and Paper Company. The Union Club, corner of Meeting and Huger streets, was a place members went for entertainment, dinner and dancing in the 1950s. Union representative Ray Gregory is pictured in the center behind the table, the others could not be identified.

Submitted by Precious Gregory

1955 Kindergarten Class ▲

Stan Mizell lived on Nassau Street when he went to kindergarten at the corner of East Bay and Amherst streets. The building, known as the Presqu'ile House, is now on the National Register of Historic Places.

Submitted by Stan Mizell

Happy Couple ▲

Roy and Evelyn Mims were married July 2, 1955 at a Methodist preacher's home near Hampton Park. The couple did not take a honeymoon because they had to go to work; Roy painted cars and Evelyn worked at the old cigar factory on the corner of Columbus and East Bay streets.

Submitted by Evelyn Mims

The Lone Star Captain ◄

Captain George Lockwood was a much-loved individual in Charleston in the mid-1950s. After he retired as a harbor pilot he enjoyed sailing his schooner, The Lone Star. Often he took groups of teenagers out with him on his boat to watch regattas.

Submitted by Leslie D. (Sister) Rutledge

Ashley Hall Stables ◄

Ronnie Friend rode horses at Ashley Hall Riding Stables, at the end of Orange Grove Road, for three years. She is pictured here in 1957 next to her horse, Patience. Ronnie learned English riding skills from Francis Thornhill, the owner of the stables.

Submitted by Veronica Friend Wolfswinkel

Christmas Eve Merry-Makers ▶

Dec. 24, 1950 marked the 50th year the descendants of James Roland Moseley and Mary Whalen Moseley gathered to celebrate Christmas at Ford Rivers' home at 4 Hagood Ave. The tradition, which began in 1900, continued through the year 2000, marking their 100th reunion.

Submitted by Elizabeth Rivers

Teenage Beat on WCSC-TV

This photo of Mel Smith (left) and Jack Petit, Jr. was taken in May 1957 to promote a local teen dance show. Both boys were teens themselves; Mel attended the High School of Charleston and Jack attended Moultrie High. WCSC-TV was located at 485 East Bay St. at that time; the address is now occupied by Luden's.

Submitted by Melvyn B. Smith

Snapshot of the Future

In 1950, Mary D. Hair, Ginny Hair and Tommy McMillan paraded around the High Battery with toy rifles and a pennant that read, "The Citadel Goes Co-Ed." The threesome drew a crowd back then, but nothing compared to the attention Shannon Faulkner garnered when she entered the Corps of Cadets on Aug. 15, 1995. The Citadel has been coeducational since that time.

Submitted by Louise McMillan

The Perfect Porch

Lucretia Mary Rowand Murphy and her husband George Patrick Lawrence Murphy built their home at 775 Rutledge Ave. Her husband passed away in 1944; Mrs. Murphy rented rooms in her home to supplement her income. She is pictured on the porch in the 1950s. The house is still a residence today.

Submitted by Chet Nowak

1960s

All Smiles on Graduation Day

Sixth-grader Mark Ziman (center) looks happy to have completed his elementary school training at Albermarle Elementary School. The school was located at the corner of Magnolia and Sycamore in West Ashley; the building still exists but is no longer a school. Ms. Hazel, his teacher, is taking care of some last-minute school business before wishing the class of 1964 a fond farewell.

Submitted by Susan Ziman

Proud Students ◄

Few things come close to the pride a child feels when he or she graduates from kindergarten. This First Baptist Church of North Charleston Class of 1966 and their teachers, Mrs. Crosby and Mrs. Dye, reflect that pride in the class picture. The only child who could be identified is Donnie Carpenter, on the far left, sitting on the floor.

Submitted by Elizabeth Abbey

A Couple of Prize Bantams ▷

Charleston High Football Coach Jack Adams proudly stands between Denny Patrick (left) and Kenny Rhea, in February 1960. The three were part of an Awards Banquet that was held at the Everett Restaurant on King Street. Patrick won the Sportsmanship trophy and Rhea won the Most Valuable Player Award.

Submitted by Dianne Patrick Dyches

Family Shrimping Business ◄

Friends and family of Thomas Backman celebrated the christening of his solid fiberglass shrimp boat, Backman Enterprise. The boat was one of six at one time; now there are two, docked 2 ½ miles from Folly Beach on James Island. Backman has been in the shrimp business for 47 years. In that time he has seen many changes in the shrimping industry, including the escalating expense of diesel fuel.

Submitted by Thomas Backman

Luxury Transportation ▲

Robert and Julia Dent are photographed in front of
their 1959 Chevrolet on Carol Street, James Island, in
1963. These models cost around $3,000 when they hit
the market. The Dents lived in the West Ashley area
but were visiting Robert's sister for Sunday dinner.

Submitted by Irene Bennett

Former Johnston Sisters Singers ▲

These Singing Sisters, who became local favorites
in the late '50s on Channel 2's "The Old Country
Church," got together in 1962 for a family dinner at
Juanita Johnston's house on Sumner Avenue. They
shared good food and conversation—and possibly a
song or two before the girls got their supper. Pictured
(left to right) are: Ruth, Louise, Lois, Kitty and Nita
Johnston.

Submitted by Lois Johnston Chears

Little Helping Hands in the Kitchen ◄

Sally (Wilensky) Magdovitz was 5 years old in 1965,
but that was old enough to help the Rev. Ella W. Brown
with the Thanksgiving meal. Ella, or "Nursie" as the
children called her, worked for the family from 1944
until 1999. They are pictured here in the kitchen of the
family home, 60 Murray Blvd.

Submitted by Rosemary R. Cohen

Charleston's Finest ▼

Sgt. Anthony Esposito and Cpl. Hoap Reeves of the
Charleston City Police Department Traffic Division
were photographed in 1962 outside Edwards 5 & 10
Cents Store, corner of King and Morris streets.

Submitted by Kathy Reeves Howe

Patriotic Princesses ▲

The girls were dressed in red, white and blue for an occasion at The Citadel in
1967. Their father, M. John "Johnny" Droze is a graduate. Pictured left to right are:
Lorrie, Regina, Dolly and Peggy Lee Droze.

Submitted by Peggy Droze

New Bus Station ▼

"Lady Greyhound" was on hand for the Grand Opening of Southern Greyhound Lines Bus Terminal on Society Street in 1966. Bus service in major cities exceeded commercial airlines and passenger railroads in the 1960s. By the 1980s, however, Charleston was among many cities that had seen a dramatic loss of service due in large part to interstate construction and the decline of neighborhoods near major bus stations.

Submitted by Cecil Kearse

Clowing Around ▲

Glen (left) and Chuck Chears smile for the camera as they have their photograph taken at their grandparents' house. The two clowns were prepared to attend the North Charleston Church of God Halloween party in 1968.

Submitted by Lois Johnston Chears

Lazy Days

Bobby Wilson was dating Linda Smith (pictured) in August 1960. He borrowed the radio shown above and the two went to Folly Beach for the day. The pier is clearly visible, with its large open area where bands played on the weekends. A jukebox provided dance music at other times. Wilson had just graduated from Chicora and Linda was attending North Charleston High School.

Submitted by Bobby Wilson

ID Tags ▶

Susan Ziman's father traveled during the week. On one of his trips in 1964 he had these sweatshirts made as gifts for everyone. Bubbles is Susan and Mark's mother. The family lived in East Oak Forest, West Ashley.

Submitted by Susan Ziman

Cocktails on the Piazza ▲

It was the custom of Ruth and Elizabeth Thames in the late 1960s to serve old fashioneds made with Southern Comfort every Sunday prior to dinner. Their cook, Janie, prepared and served dinner, which usually consisted of fried chicken, rice and gravy, okra or green beans, tomatoes, celery and biscuits. Iced tea was served at dinner, along with seasonal fruit pies. Their home, at 64 Hasell St., is now owned by The Indigo Inn. Pictured left to right: Donald Watson Thames, Jack Connard Thames, Janet Thames and Florence Thames.

Submitted by Anne Thames

Playtime in the Park ◄
Suzzette Nowak and her mother-in-law Lucretia took baby Celeste in her stroller to Hampton Park one afternoon in the mid-'60s. Celeste's father Chet drove everyone in his 1956 Ford Fairlane—the first car he ever owned. He bought it in 1963 for $350.

Submitted by Chet Nowak

Bishops Beaten By Rocks ▶
Mike Young, a guard for the Battling Bishops, keeps control of the ball while keeping Alan Coleman, #44 of the St. Andrews Rocks, at arm's distance during a tight game. It was the early '60s; Coleman was a junior and said the game that night was by far the best he'd ever played. The Bishops ended up losing by one point, but went on to beat the Rocks by 33 points in a tournament a few weeks later. Bishops finished the season 23-1 and won the AA State Championship.

Submitted by Mike Young

Annual Banquet ▲

The Charleston Retail Merchants' Association members held a banquet each year at Coburg Dairy. Pictured here in 1964 (left to right) are: Leon Fulmer, president of the merchants' association, Sen. Rembert C. Dennis, Rep. James N. Condon and Russell L. Powell.

Submitted by Tom Fulmer

Folly, Fish, Food ◄

Suzette and Chet Nowak were newlyweds in May 1965 when they took a picnic and went fishing at Folly. The coupled lived in an apartment on King Street at the time. Nowak worked for Western Electric Company.

Submitted by Chet Nowak

Winter Wonderland ▼

When the temperatures dropped below freezing, L. Louis Green, III turned a sprinkler on. In the morning his three daughters awoke to an icicle forest on the shrubs in the yard at 75 South Battery. Louisa (Green) Fisher (left), and sisters Frederica and Dorothy, are pictured here in the 1960s, enjoying yard sicles.

Submitted by Frederica Mathewes-Green

Condons Celebrate 50 Years—of Marriage ▲

In 1965 both the personal and professional lives of the Condons were flourishing; William Francis Condon and his wife Caroline Igoe Condon celebrated 50 years of marriage at the Fort Sumter Hotel. Their business, opened as a fabric store by James F. Condon in 1896, had expanded to include sons Matthew A. and William F. Condon. In 1948 the store grew across King Street to Warren Street, with a connecting breezeway over John Street.

Submitted by Betty Rosen

Citadel Camp ▲

Gen. Mark Clark initiated summer camps in 1957 to encourage boys to consider The Citadel for their higher education. Two sessions, both led by Citadel cadets, were held: the first for local boys and the second for out-of-town boys whose school year ended later. The boys stayed in barracks, played athletics, toured the historical sites of Charleston and spent time at The Citadel Beach House. The Citadel discontinued summer residential camps in 2006. Pictured here in 1967 (first row, second from the right) is John McQueen Copeland.

Submitted by Mary McQueen

Immaculate Conception Student ▲

Maxine Brown was a high school student at Immaculate Conception School on Coming Street in 1963. After graduation she attended Roper School of Practical Nursing, completing her nursing education in 1972. With her nursing credentials she worked at Roper Hospital. She retired from Roper as a surgical nurse.

Submitted by Maxine Poindexter

Baptist College Cheerleaders ◀

Baptist College, now Charleston Southern University, moved to the new campus in North Charleston in 1966. The dormitories weren't ready at that time, so students lived in trailers. Pictured here are the school's cheerleaders (left to right): Joy Pengra, Ginger Thornley, Merrily Spence, Lynn (Cromer) Mauldin, Jan Royal, Anna (Wireman) McAllister, Carol Odom, Carol (Meade) Coopman.

Submitted by Anna Wireman McAllister

Murray High School "Tigers" ▷

For the first time in the school's history, Murray Vocational School won the lower state basketball championship during the 1962-63 school year. Their athletic banquet, pictured here, was held at the Plantation Restaurant. Chubby Baker won the West End Dairy Trophy for Best Player in the Lowcountry. Murray, located on Chisholm Street off Broad Street, was an all-boys' school until the 1950s. The building is now apartments. Front row (left to right): Eddie Banks, Rick Maull, Larry Dandridge, Joe Parker, Chubby Baker, Donald Morillo. Back row: Harvey Blanchard, coach, Jimmy Kittrell, Jimmy Hooks, Frank Mathis, Edward White, Leroy Veno.

Submitted by Donald O. Morillo, Sr.

Best of Both Worlds ▲

As children in 1969 Libby (left) and Ellen Leland had the best of both worlds: they grew up on a farm on Wadmalaw Island, and they enjoyed "city life" as well, attending Ashley Hall. Pictured in the background are Bandit, the spotted horse on the left, and the girls' father's childhood horse Champ on the right. Champ is now buried under the live oak tree in the photo. Their pet deer, Tagalong, was abandoned by his mother in the farm's grain fields. He was returned to the wild.

Submitted by Daisy Barron Leland

Silver Christmas Tree

The Petits lived on Birch Street in Whipper Barony in 1960; silver Christmas trees were all the rage during that decade and have made a comeback as "retro" decorations in recent years. Susan (left) was about 15 years old and her sister Linda was about 17. Both girls went to Chicora High School.

Submitted by Linda Lassiter

Fine Kettle of Fish ◄

Tony Balzano went fishing every day before work, weather permitting. He worked in the composing room at *The News and Courier*, and retired after more than 50 years of service. He is pictured here in 1960 with a mess of spot tails caught in the Bohicket River behind his house on Johns Island.

Submitted by Toni Kirby

Condon's Children's Shoe Department ▲

On the second floor of Condon's Department Store downtown in the 1960s there was a magical place where children tried on shoes. The carousel did not turn, but it didn't really matter. It was still great fun to sit on the lion, or the elephant, or the rhino while grown-ups measured and laced and buckled and generally fussed over you while you were trying to play.

Submitted by Merrile M. Kinard

Double Celebration ▲

Ritchie (left) and Stevie Weil loved visiting their grandfather Julius Weil at his home at 112 South Battery. The boys were celebrating Grandaddy's 61st birthday and Hannakah in December, 1968. Family celebrations were usually wonderful, lively dinners such as the one depicted here in the Weil dining room.

Submitted by Alice Weil

Miss Murray Contestant ◄

Toya Drose didn't win in 1960, but she did place in the contest. All female students were welcome to participate in the contest at Murray Vocational High School. The event was held in the gymnasium. Toya was 17 years old at the time.

Submitted by Sally Ott

Rite of Passage: The Two-Wheeler
Skipper Ott was 5 years old when he got his first bicycle in 1968. His family lived at 8 Sothel Ave., in Byrnes Downs.
Submitted by David Ott